LORD ASHFIELD AND COLONEL E. T. BROOK, C.B.E.

SEVEN BATTALIONS

The story of

LONDON TRANSPORT'S HOME GUARD

1940 — 1946

The Naval & Military Press Ltd

Published by

The Naval & Military Press Ltd
Unit 10 Ridgewood Industrial Park,
Uckfield, East Sussex,
TN22 5QE England

Tel: +44 (0) 1825 749494
Fax: +44 (0) 1825 765701

www.naval-military-press.com
www.nmarchive.com

COLONEL E. T. BROOK, C.B.E.

CONTENTS

LONDON PASSENGER TRANSPORT BOARD

Telephone

This book has been written so that we may have a record of some of the life of the L.P.T.B. Home Guard, and so that we may, in moments of leisure, read it and so bring back to our memories happenings with which so many of us have been connected.

As I look back over the war years incidents in the life of the Unit pour into my mind. They illustrate moments of stress or of danger, the problems of organisation or the every-day happenings that made the existence of London Transport Home Guard. All have one thing in common, the spirit of comradeship and service which I consider had few equals in any unit in the entire Home Guard. This spirit will mean much more to all of us as the years pass. I count it a great honour to have been in command of the Unit from start to finish. My task was much lightened by the support I received from every Officer, N.C.O. and man of the Unit, and it was this support that enabled me to overcome so many of the difficulties we met. I thank all Ranks for this as it did much to make the Unit efficient. My thanks are also extended to the auxiliaries for the assistance they gave.

The times are still full of difficulty but, good times or ill, I know that you as Home Guards have the spirit and the will to conquer any difficulty. I wish all of you health and prosperitybut, above all, that deep sense of solid satisfaction which comes of having served King and Country to the utmost in the hour of need.

P. J. Brooke.

The story that is told in this book represents
one of the outstanding achievements of the staff of the
Board during the war years, reflecting the highest
credit on all those who participated, involving as
it did, the sacrifice of so much of what might
otherwise have been leisure time in order to serve
this country in its time of need.

I have seen the Unit from time to time on parade,
in difficult exercises and on ceremonial occasions
and have their always reflected in the rapid progress
made from a humble start to a highly efficient
Unit which could only have been achieved by the
extraordinary enthusiasm of the Officers and men.
This service in a common cause provided an
excellent opportunity for the staff to really get
to know one another, and I know that the
spirit of camaraderie among all ranks
was very high. May this spirit long
continue in the days of peace.

Ashfield

1 *The First Year*

LONDON Transport's Home Guard Unit began as an order, a simple thing, just a plain command to start. It was given to Mr. E. T. Brook, Superintendent of Rolling Stock (Railways) and Chairman of the A.R.P. Committee, on May 28, 1940—two weeks after Mr. Anthony Eden had appealed by radio to every man between 17 and 65 to join a force to be known as the Local Defence Volunteers. The order given to Mr. Brook called for the formation of a London Transport L.D.V. Group, and there was a passing mention of organisation too. Anything less suggestive of what the Unit was to become and mean could barely be imagined.

Mr. Brook decided that he had better join the L.D.V. himself first, so, with Mr. A. W. M. Mawby and Mr. J. A. Wilks, First and Second Assistant Superintendents of Rolling Stock, (Railways) he signed on at London District Headquarters and was given the power to appoint organisers. Mr. Brook found six and made each responsible for a department. They were Messrs. L. B. Hewitt (Trams and Trolleybuses), R. F. Morkill (Civil Engineers), P. L. Smith (Railways and Administrative), F. H. Wigner (Electrical Engineers), W. A. C. Snook (Buses and Coaches), and A. W. M. Mawby (Chief Mechanical Engineers).

Mr. Wilks was Assistant Organiser under Mr. Brook ; and when Mr. Mawby was made Second in Command his place was taken by Mr. R. A. Arthurton. Later, Mr. Snook was replaced by Mr. J. H. Williams.

By this time everyone in the Board's employ had heard about the Group and hundreds of applications to join came in every day.

Headquarters were at Acton works and the orderly room was Mr. Mawby's own office with a staff of two civilians, an adjutant and a clerk. This organisation had to try to issue to everyone who joined a properly signed card of membership and at the same time give to the police full details of every man for checking purposes. As the ordinary work of the London Transport was carried on as well, the organisers were busy till after midnight every day. Difficulties sprouted in all directions, but the Group began to take shape.

In those days there were no normal ranks for officers. When Mr. Mawby became a Staff Officer on July 17, 1940, he wore the four blue bars of a Group Commander on the shoulder straps of his battledress. This appointment was made four days before the first parade which was held before Lord Ashfield. Among those present were Brigadier Symons, C.M.G., Lord Denham, M.C. and Col. McLean of London Headquarters. Some 2,500 men were on parade, but with the exception of a picked guard of honour, which wore denim uniform, most had only

the blue and grey of London Transport with an L.D.V. armlet. There were no rifles.

After the inspection Lord Ashfield complimented the men on their smart and soldierly bearing. He said, 'Having in mind the recent formation of this unit and the very limited opportunities you have had for drill, what I have seen this morning is particularly gratifying, and I am indeed proud of my association with the unit. More than 15,000 of our staff have responded to the call. Each day there is an increase in the number of volunteers, and very soon we shall have not only one of the largest but, I firmly believe, one of the finest, if not the very finest, units in this country. I and my colleagues on the Board are indeed proud of this achievement—and yet it is only what we had expected of our staff, who have at all times rendered devoted service to the public.'

Lord Ashfield then paid high tribute to Mr. Brook who, he said, devoted himself day and night to his task and was the ideal man for the job, full of drive and energy and enthusiastic to a degree.

'What we have we hold,' declared Lord Ashfield. 'Our motto is "Strong for Service"; strong for service in time of peace and trebly strong when all you and I have striven to create over more years than we care to recall, and on which we depend for our livelihood, is threatened with destruction. We are prepared to defend such things with our lives.'

Every Home Guard in the service of the Board looks back on that parade with a feeling of pride and satisfaction. They knew then, as one of the men was heard to say, 'We are in on something BIG'. Proof came two days later—July 23, 1940—when Mr. Churchill, in one of his brilliant broadcasts, changed the name of the L.D.V. to the Home Guard, a name which became, almost in a night, a symbol of Britain's resistance.

Even more speed was put into the shaping of London Transport Home Guard. The Board agreed to the release for full-time service of six Battalion Commanders, as follows : No. 1 (Railways), Mr. T. H. P. Peerless ; No. 2 (Administrative, C.M.E. and

Generating Stations), Mr. S. G. Lane ; No. 3 (Busmen—North of the Thames), Mr. H. K. Cleary ; No. 4 (Busmen—South of the Thames), Mr. T. H. Powell ; No. 5 (Southern Trams and Trolleybuses), Mr. E. R. Alford ; No. 6 (Northern Trams and Trolleybuses), Mr. A. L. Coucher.

Mr. Brook was Group Commander over all with Mr. Mawby as Staff Officer. These battalions, some far too large by normal standards, were based on the Board's organisation rather than on areas chosen for a strict military purpose. This was done to add more speed and because the duty of the Home Guard in those days was solely to watch for parachute troops and to protect vital points. In the Board's area, of course, there were hundreds of targets of great importance—garages, stations, power plants, works—and all had to be guarded constantly every night. Nobody knew if the enemy contemplated a ' suicide squad ' attack on London's transport system, and

all the Home Guard could do was remain on the alert continuously. It was a trying job in all weathers for men, at that time, in no position to defend themselves or the property they were set to protect. There still was a tragic shortage of weapons and everything regular troops count as essential and take for granted. Only enthusiasm and willingness to serve were on the plus side.

Battalion Commanders had a specially hard time, for then the officers under them all had to do a normal day's work for the Board as well as their service duties. The problems were multiplied because most of the Board's employees were shift workers, free for Home Guard duty at one hour in one week and at a quite different hour in the next week. In spite of this, each battalion had to be organised in companies consisting of 15 or more sections each at a garage or station or depot. Some of these sections in the same battalion were as much as 40 miles apart.

Looking back on the 3rd Batt., as an example, one finds a total strength of 5,000 split up into A and B Coys. with about 2,000 each, and C Coy. with 1,000. Later, whole battalions were smaller than some of these companies, and the wonder is that the Home Guard prospered so greatly in spite of what then was a thicket of tangled organisation. That it did prosper was due to selfless work by all concerned and sterling support from the Board. At that time odd rooms and disused tramcars were the stores and guard-rooms ; it was all clearly inadequate, so Mr. Brook set about co-ordinating requests for better premises and then finding the buildings and fitting them up. Modern guardrooms and strong points were provided and certain railway units were given con-verted coaches on sidings. In all, the Board built or converted 137 guardrooms and 76 strong points, while 12 railway coaches were adapted for use. Mr. Brook, after much

thought, applied to the Board for the release of many men for full-time Home Guard duty, and Lord Ashfield and his colleagues granted the request. This, perhaps more than any other move, set the unit firmly on its feet.

Specially chosen men took lessons in guerilla warfare, the backbone of training in the summer of 1940, from such able instruc-tors as Tom Wintringham and Hugh Slater, at Osterley Park and later, in larger numbers, from Lieut. Col. Pollock at Denbies, Dorking, the school which set the standard for all Home Guard training. As the Battle of Britain raged over S.E. England the all-round enthusiasm and spirited leadership increased in intensity. By December 1940 London Transport Home Guard was already the envy of many other units. When, in that month, the Duke of Kent visited the Windsor, Hanwell and Victoria garages to inspect the men he declared that he was much impressed by what he saw.

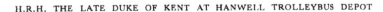

H.R.H. THE LATE DUKE OF KENT AT HANWELL TROLLEYBUS DEPOT

2 *Unit Headquarters*

In 1941 the Home Guard was transformed from a civilian army without uniform and with very few weapons into a real military force. Greatcoats and battledress, which had first appeared with London Transport in August 1940, steadily increased in quantity, steel helmets came spasmodically, but rifles were now being collected from the Tower of London by the lorry-load. A few Thompson sub-machine guns accompanied the rifles from the United States ; in April the much-maligned pikes were issued, followed by Browning automatic rifles, machine guns, anti-tank missiles and bombs ; Northover projectors preceded the Spigot mortars. The Home Guard could now say they were really able to guard London Transport property as they kept watch in the night. Training developed an intensity not previously known.

Battalion Commanders became Lieut. Colonels, Company Commanders became Majors and Platoon Commanders received the rank of Lieutenant. The badge of London Transport was the ' other ranks ' badge of the King's Royal Rifle Corps, which some had worn as Regular Army soldiers in the 1914-18 war or even earlier. These ' second time ' men were able to instruct their colleagues in the great traditions of the K.R.R.C.

Mr. Brook became Officer Commanding the entire unit with the rank of Colonel ; Second in Command was Lieut. Col. Mawby ; Majors Saville and Duffell, as Home Guard staff officers Q and A respectively, were given General Service commissions with the rank of Captain.

So that he could devote more time to the Home Guard Col. Brook relinquished his appointment with London Transport as Superintendent of Rolling Stock (Railways). The Home Guard Headquarters was moved from Acton, to 32, Westbourne Terrace, Paddington, and Group Headquarters opened there on May 20, 1943.

While these changes were being made an officers' mess was opened in Baker Street, and was available to all officers of the entire unit ; Capt. Randall was Mess Secretary. The first important night there was on January 7, 1943, when Lord Ashfield paid an informal visit. He was received by Col. Brook and many officers, with some of whom he played darts. Lord Ashfield visited the mess on February 24, 1943, and met officers unable to be present when he first went there. Lord Ashfield was accompanied by Mr. T. E. Thomas, and many officers of the Board, on this occasion. Later the mess was moved to Westbourne Terrace and was most efficiently run.

By this time there had been more battalion changes ; on and after March 1941 they had been re-numbered as the 41st to 46th County of London and soon there came a seventh battalion—the 60th London. The remarkable thing all through was the way in which ceiling strengths were maintained and enthusiasm and team spirit continued to develop. Specialised sub-units were formed, training schools opened and numbers of men went to Bisley every Sunday for firing practice. In Central London bomb damaged buildings were used for instruction in street fighting.

As the part of the Home Guard in the defence of London grew in importance it became necessary to re-plan the London Transport Unit. Col. Brook and Lieut. Col. Mawby completed a big reorganisation scheme which resulted in all battalions conforming as nearly as possible to Home Guard Zone boundaries. The newly formed 60th London Batt. was placed under the command of Lieut. Col. J. B. Woodward ; the Central area was taken over by the

43rd Batt. ; the 42nd and 44th were stationed south of the Thames ; and the remaining four battalions covered the northern half of the capital. During the reorganisation, whole platoons and even companies were moved from one battalion to another, and for the first time bus, trolleybus and railway men and administrative staff were intermingled in the same unit. This reorganisation was so successful that it earned official approval and congratulations and no further changes of a material kind were ever made.

Occasionally Sunday morning exercises and drills were varied by holding church parades. Throughout the history of the London Transport Home Guard, church parades proved very popular and were always well attended.

Three battalions, the 41st, 43rd and 44th, had padres attached to them. The padre of the 41st Batt. was the Rev. C. Tatham, O.C.F. The Rev. Anthony Toller, B.D., was attached to the 44th and with the 43rd was the Rev. S. Osborne Goodchild, A.K.C.

A regular feature of the 44th Batt.'s activities was their church parades. The first of these was held on September 28, 1941, when the battalion paraded some 400 strong at Flanders Barracks, Flodden Road, Camberwell. Before marching to St. Giles Church, Camberwell, the Group Commander inspected the parade and presented two members of the battalion with Meritorious Service Certificates.

The priest in charge, the Rev. Anthony Toller, selected the lesson which was read by the C.O., Lieut. Col. Powell. It was taken from the Book of Nehemiah, and despite the fact that it was written more than 2,000 years ago, it might have been specially prepared for the Home Guard, as those who care to consult their Bibles may see for themselves. It was indeed an exhortation to the Home Guard of Jerusalem of those days. The padre then gave the first of those addresses which were to become so well known to men of the 44th.

H.Q. OFFICERS

COLONEL E. T. BROOK, INSPECTING THE GUARD OUTSIDE WESTMINSTER ABBEY— NOVEMBER 11TH

SENIOR OFFICERS OF THE UNIT

MAJOR-GENERAL VISCOUNT BRIDGEMAN, C.B.,
D.S.O., M.C., WITH THE UNIT COMMANDER

The 43rd's first Church Parade was held at Christ Church, Turnham Green, for the annual Remembrance Day Service. The parade was headed by the battalion band under the directorship of Lieut. A. E. Ashcroft. Col. Brook presented Proficiency Certificates to 200 N.C.O.s and men.

On May 14, 15 and 16, 1941, the Home Guard provided the King's Guard at Buckingham Palace and St. James's Palace. The 1st London (Westminster) Batt. supplied the guard. F Coy. of the 2nd L.P.T.B. Batt., based at 55, Broadway, had formed a close friendship with No. 1 Coy. of the 1st London, and this resulted in F Coy. receiving an invitation to join the 1st London Batt. in mounting the guard. The men chosen were specially trained by the Guards sergeants at Wellington Barracks. They gave up hours of their time to become movement perfect. Great crowds watched them all through the period of the guard, which was carried out with a soldierly bearing and accuracy which earned the highest praise.

ROLL OF UNIT H.Q. OFFICERS AT 'STAND DOWN'

Names and Ranks	Appointment
Col. E. T. Brook, C.B.E.	Unit Commander
Lieut. Col. G. Morgan Evans	Medical Adviser
Major R. F. Morkill, M.C.	A & Q
Major L. B. Hewitt	A & Q
Capt. W. H. Johnson	Intelligence and H.Q. Platoon
Capt. A. J. Webb	M.L.O.
Capt. H. G. R. Stevenson	P.A.D.
Capt. A. E. Courtnell	P.A.D.
Capt. J. W. F. Scott	Transport
Capt. K. Shave	Engineer
Capt. W. Drew	W.T.O.
Lieut. C. E. Watters	A & Q
Lieut. H. H. C. Barton	Signals
Lieut. S. T. Tilby	Liaison
2nd Lt. H. Allen	2 i/c H.Q. Platoon

Deceased

Lieut. Col. A. W. M. Mawby, O.B.E., T.D., D.L.   Unit 2 i/c

3 Parades and Training

ANOTHER milestone in the history of the London Transport Group was reached on June 7, 1941, when they celebrated their first anniversary at a parade at the Sports Ground at Osterley. Brigadier Whitehead, C.B., C.M.G., C.B.E., D.S.O., Commander of the Home Guard, London District, accompanied by Lord Ashfield, Col. Brook and Col. Symons, inspected the Board's Unit.

All battalions were represented and the parade was under the command of Lieut. Col. Mawby. Really first-rate marching was seen and colour was added to the proceedings by the Group band under Lieut. Monk, which was making its first appearance. Brigadier Whitehead, addressing the great parade, congratulated all the officers and men on their smartness, while Lord Ashfield pointed out that perseverance and undaunted en- thusiasm had in 12 months completely transformed a volunteer force into an efficient military unit—so outstanding that he and his colleagues on the Board took very great pride in the Unit, which they considered to be their own.

Less than two years after London Trans-

BRIGADIER C. WHITEHEAD, C.B., C.M.G., INSPECTING THE 46TH BATTALION

port's Group was formed the fine training centre at Chiswick was opened for the 43rd Batt. This centre, originally a sports ground, was badly damaged during the blitz. When Lieut. Col. H. K. Cleary took over, officers and other ranks co-operated and the pavilion was re-decorated, the electric light restored and the hot-water system for the changing rooms put into working order. The ground was laid out to include a bombing range and an assault course, and there was plenty of space for general training and drill. Waste ground nearby became a special range for anti-tank weapons. The ground was opened in the presence of Col. Brook and Col. T. G. Dalby, C.B., D.S.O., Commander of F Zone, who saw the men at work on various methods of training, particularly Northover Projectors, firing S.I.P.s and also Spigot mortars, both of which weapons were used with considerable accuracy. After these demonstrations Lieut. Col. Cleary spoke of the good work which had been performed by men of the 43rd in clearing the wilderness and weeds and bringing the ground up to excellent condition.

The Chiswick training centre was gradually improved. Tents were obtained and the cookhouse restored. Every week a number of men lived there under canvas from Saturday afternoon until Sunday evening and experienced the same parades, drills and conditions of life as troops of the Regular Army. On July 18, 1942, a second training centre was opened at Stanmore by Col. Brook. This centre had been organised by Lieut. Col. Coucher, Major Cameron and Capt. Wheeler of the 46th Batt. and was mainly intended to be a centre for the use of that battalion. Wooden huts, with adequate kitchen arrangements where good meals could be cooked, were provided and here, too, many men went at weekends for special courses of training. It was decided that Chiswick and Stanmore must serve a wider purpose, and on April 3, 1943, both establishments were officially re-opened as the Unit North and South Training Camps, although actually the South Camp had been available to all battalions for some months.

Capt. F. C. Rainbird became South Camp Commandant and Major C. W. Wheeler Commandant of North Camp. Lieut. Gen.

Sir Arthur Smith, G.O.C. London District, paid an official visit to the South Camp accompanied by Lieut. Col. Longueville. The G.O.C. made a thorough inspection, paying particular attention to the large number of squads under instruction. Tribute must be paid to the generosity and kindness of Mr. J. Musgrave of Messrs. Richard Crittall & Company. The repeated help given to both camps by the supply of plant for the preparation of food resulted in the attainment of a very high standard.

On completion of the second year of the Home Guard men from every unit in the London District paraded in Hyde Park, where the King took the salute as they started on their march through the West End. Over 5,000 troops participated, making a column nearly 3,000 yds. in length. Each L.P.T.B. Batt. was represented by two officers and 30 other ranks. The Home Guards were honoured to receive a special message from the King. It stated : ' The second year in the life of the Home Guard, which ends today, has been one of marked and continuous progress. I have watched with satisfaction the growing efficiency of the Force in training, equipment and co-operation with the Regular Army as well as the Civil Defence Services. Many of the original Volunteers have by now unavoidably left the Home Guard and

many have joined the Regular Forces. They leave behind them a great tradition of service and comradeship which will inspire the new recruits now enrolling for the defence of their country. Whatever the coming year may bring, I know that the Home Guard will offer the fiercest resistance to any enemy who may set foot on these shores, and that its members will spare no efforts to make

themselves ever more ready for battle.

'In order to mark my appreciation of the services given by the Home Guard with such devotion and perseverance, I have today assumed the appointment of Colonel-in-Chief of the Force ; and I send my best wishes to all its members.'

The second anniversary parade of the L.P.T.B. Unit was held at the South Training Camp on Sunday, May 31, 1942. The inspection was conducted by Brigadier Whitehead, and music was provided by the Unit band, 43rd Batt. band and a pipe band provided by the 43rd Batt. After the inspection Brigadier Whitehead commented on the soldierly bearing of the men and their increased efficiency. The march past was led by the 41st Batt. and then units of the 42nd Batt. gave a demonstration of mobile column work, including embussing and debussing. Northover Projectors were fired by men of the 60th and the Spigot mortar was demonstrated by a team commanded by Lieut. Johnson of Group H.Q. At a range of 200 yds. a tank was hit three times out of four.

In May 1943 the Home Guard again provided the King's Guard at Buckingham Palace and St. James's and, as before, men from London Transport were included. As a result of the reorganisation the task was now in the hands of the 43rd Batt. and once again selected men gave up much of their time to the specialised training under Guards N.C.O.s at Wellington Barracks. Again large crowds turned out to see their Home Guard, and the 'slow march' was as good as, if not better than, on the previous occasion.

The 1943 anniversary parade was held in the historical cockpit in Hyde Park, a unique honour. Lieut. Gen. Sir Arthur Smith inspected the seven battalions which paraded—well over 3,000 all ranks—the only Home Guard unit ever to parade annually in the famous cockpit. Once again Lieut. Col. Mawby was in command of the parade, with R.S.M. Lavery as Parade R.S.M. The Guard of Honour was supplied by C Coy. of the 45th Batt. and commanded by Capt. W. H. Johnson of Unit H.Q.

The organisation necessary to ensure that each battalion arrived from its assembly area in the park in its proper order and at the exact time was facilitated by the use of field wireless with a central control in the cockpit. This service was provided by the 60th Batt., who were completely equipped with R.T. During the parade a short service was conducted by the Rev. A. Toller. The music for the march past was provided by the Unit band, 43rd Batt. band, and the 44th Batt. band, under Capt. E. J. Bates. Lord Ashfield and Col. Brook were on the base when the salute was taken by Lieut. Gen. Sir Arthur Smith.

During 1943 it was decided that all H.Q.

BIRTHDAY PARADE, HYDE PARK, 1943

personnel should wear a distinguishing flash. The design finally approved consisted of a blue circle intersected by a red lightning flash with the letters ' L.T.', one on each side of the flash. The design was mounted on a white background with black diagonal lines. By this time H.Q. staff had reached larger proportions. While H.Q. had been at Acton no trouble was experienced in providing a guard, but with the removal to Westbourne Terrace it became necessary to make special arrangements and each battalion was called upon to provide a guard in rotation. This was not entirely satisfactory owing to the long distances some men had to travel. Finally the H.Q. platoon was found from men from several battalions. The platoon was placed under the command of Unit H.Q. Intelligence Officer, Capt. W. H. Johnson.

The training of the London Transport Unit as a whole was greatly encouraged by the action of a number of the Board's Officers in presenting Challenge Cups for contests within the battalion. The Cups were presented by : Mr. H. J. Green—Chief Engineer (Civil), Mr. J. H. Parker—Chief Electrical Engineer, Mr. V. A. M. Robertson —Engineer-in-Chief, Mr. S. R. Geary— Operating Manager (Central Buses), Mr. W. A. C. Snook—Acting Chief Engineer (Buses and Coaches), and Col. Brook—Unit Commander.

Each Cup was presented to a particular battalion for contests within that battalion.

In addition, Col. Brook presented a trophy for an annual inter-battalion contest. Each battalion was required to enter a battle platoon. The competition, a combination of ceremonial inspection and turn out, marching by map and compass, field tactical exercises, and range discipline, finished with range firing at 200 yds. ; it was moulded on the lines of the well known X Sector N.F. event. The contest was held in and around Hedgerley Park by permission of Col. P. E. Colman, C.B.E., D.S.O., M.C., X Sector Commander, who also provided the judges

B

LIEUTENANT-GENERAL SIR ARTHUR SMITH TAKING THE SALUTE

THE PARADE SERVICE

and umpires under the supervision of Lieut. Col. C. H. Smith, O.B.E. and Major G. Levy. The competition called for a specially high standard of all-round efficiency of officers and men and required considerable physical effort. It was attended by a very large number of officers representing London district and all sub-districts. The Cup was presented by the Director-General of the Home Guard, Major-Gen. Viscount Bridgeman, C.B., D.S.O., M.C., to Lieut. A. G. Chiles, who led the 60th battle platoon to victory.

The North Camp received a slight setback early in 1944 when the Government requisitioned the ground for other purposes. Luckily another site was soon found only a mile from the old one. Thanks to the untiring efforts of Major Wheeler and his N.C.O.s and men, this new camp became in many respects superior to the old site. The camp was opened by Brigadier Swinton, M.C. Officer Commanding N.W. London sub-district, on April 16, 1944, in the presence of many visiting officers. Lieut. Col. Powell lent the 44th Batt. band. This enabled the representative units from the 46th and 60th Batts. and three Cadet battalions to march past to the stirring strains of the Regimental March, which never failed to produce the very best from troops on parade. By arrangement with Col. Brook, this North Camp was used extensively for the training of Army Cadet battalions.

A few weeks later the fourth and last anniversary parade was held, once again in the cockpit at Hyde Park, on June 4, 1944. This was much the best ever held by the Unit. The Inspecting Officer was Gen. Sir Charles Lloyd, K.C.B., D.S.O., M.C., the newly appointed General Officer Commanding, London District. The General was met by Col. Brook. Lord Ashfield was represented by Mr. John Cliff. The G.O.C. was received with a salute by the Unit buglers under Drum Major Elles. The Guard of Honour, again commanded by Capt. Johnson, was drawn from the Unit Headquarters platoon.

The general salute by some 4,000 Home Guards and massed bands, which numbered nearly 100 instrumentalists, was given as the General reached the main formation. The parade was drawn up facing the Serpentine with the 60th on the right of the line by reason of their having won the Brook Inter-battalion Trophy. The remaining battalions stood in numerical order from 41 to 46. The seven Medical units, each led by its Medical Officers, were drawn up behind the battalions. The Wireless unit, led by Lieut. J. Wood, again controlled the assembly areas and this time formed up with the 60th for the march past. By now four bands existed in the Unit and these were all at full strength. The three battalions with bands, 41st, 43rd and 44th, marched to the cockpit headed by their own band, while the 60th, so largely responsible for forming the Unit band, were led by them. The Corps of Drums brought in the 46th Batt. The crowds this time were much larger than on previous anniversary parades, but this had been foreseen and a far greater seating area was provided on the edge of the Serpentine. Even so, many hundreds stood all round the cockpit throughout the parade which, as usual, was blessed with excellent weather. By permission of the Board a film record was made. Lieut. Dix, of the 44th Batt., organised the production, and the film was subsequently shown on many occasions and will always remain one of the few permanent records of the London Transport Home Guard.

After the inspection by the G.O.C. a service was conducted by the Rev. A. Toller, assisted by the Rev. G. Tatham. The G.O.C.'s address was extremely important— it was only two days before the launching of the invasion of France. He stated significantly that he had recently attended a very important parade, but considered the one that day no less important. The General spoke of the work done by the Home Guard with the A.A. guns and with the Civil Defence. He added, ' Today we are on the threshold of great events'. The march past followed to the music of the massed bands with the 60th leading. The 41st Batt. marched to the stirring music of their own Pipe Band. On this parade there were many important visitors, including Brigadiers A. H. Swinton, M.C., H. L. Graham, M.C., Copland-Griffiths, D.S.O., M.C., L. M. Gibbs, C.V.O., D.S.O., M.C., Colonels Sir Geoffrey Hippersley-Cox, C.B.E., G. S. Hussey, M.C. (L.M.S.), E. Marshall (L.N.E.R.), S. H. Isaac (S.R.) and T. C. Dalby, C.B., D.S.O.

General Symons, an old friend of the London Transport Unit, was also present. Officers of the Board present included : Messrs. T. E. Thomas, C.B.E., C. G. Page, M.C., S. R. Geary, O.B.E., E. Graham, W. Gott, O.B.E., H. T. Hutchings, Evan Evans, L. C. Hawkins, J. A. Wilks, W. F. Wright and J. J. McGregor.

A feature of Home Guard training was periodical route marches.

Most route marches in the Group took place on Sunday mornings and were always extremely well attended. Busmen, railmen, Board's officers, and clerks turned out in full battle order to march seven or eight miles in all conditions and weather. Here are a few reports of these route marches, selected at random :

'On Sunday, March 1st, the 60th Batt. did a six mile route march in full battle order. The column was headed by the fifes and drums of the Coldstream Guards, with the Unit band between the 2nd and 3rd Coys. With a crash of drums, the column moved from the Metropolitan Railway Athletic Ground, with Lieut. Col. Woodward leading his men. The salute was taken at Wembley Town Hall by Col. E. T. Brook, who was accompanied by the Mayor of Wembley. Nearly 700 all ranks attended and it says much for the enthusiasm of the men that they turned out early on a Sunday morning for a long march.'

'On Sunday, January 30th, the 46th Batt. paraded at North Finchley for a route march of five miles. The weather was kind and it was a glorious morning. Altogether 600 officers and other ranks, including the L.P.T.B. Home Guard Band and the Corps of Drums attended. The battalion moved off with the Corps of Drums at the head, followed by A and B Coys. Then came the Home Guard Band with C, D, E and F Coys. in order. The rear of the column was covered by a lorry mounting a machine gun for A.A. protection. The salute was taken at a point en route by Col. A. H. C. Swinton, M.C.

CAPTAIN JOHNSON WITH GUARD OF HONOUR, HYDE PARK, 1944

Also at the saluting base were Col. Brook, Lieut. Col. Mawby and a number of officers from Group H.Q. As the battalion neared the base the band played the march " Old Comrades " for the march past. The troops looked splendid and marched like veterans as indeed most of them were. Col. Swinton was complimentary on the general turnout and marching and was well pleased with the whole affair. A letter of congratulation on the fine show has been received from Col. E. T. Brook, Group Commander.'

The War Office authorised the voluntary enrolment of women auxiliary Home Guards in April 1943. The amount of very useful work undertaken by this branch of the Service was not always fully appreciated by those outside the Home Guard. This was due in some measure to the complete absence of any official uniform. The women's duties consisted mostly of clerical work, vehicle driving, cooking and telephone operating— work which was often performed under difficult conditions during field exercises, but always with a cheerful countenance and considerable adaptability. The figure of women in the strength of the Unit stood consistently at about 200.

The allocation of Permanent Staff Instructors from the Regular Army contributed very largely to the steady improvement and constant enthusiasm. All battalions had one P.S.I., but more were allocated according to battalion tasks and strengths.

By 1944 the Unit contained 14 Permanent Staff Instructors. Many of them gave up hours of their free time to lecture and train their men in various subjects so that they, in turn, could themselves become specialists. The nature of the Board's organisation resulted inevitably in company and platoon headquarters of various battalions being widespread. It was therefore difficult for Battalion Commanders to visit these headquarters. To solve this difficulty the Board

generously placed eight private cars at the disposal of the Home Guard. These were relicensed under the G scheme and proved invaluable.

During the summer of 1940 the London Transport Rifle Club began an ambitious programme for the small-bore training of the Home Guard. In addition to the permanent ranges already in use, many temporary ranges were constructed at convenient points throughout Greater London. Capt. W. Drew, the Club Secretary, worked unceasingly for this all-important cause ; 88 Club rifles, in addition to Capt. Drew's own rifles, were placed at the disposal of the Board's Home Guard. The crowning achievement in the early days was the purchase, made by the far-seeing Secretary, of 500,000 rounds of American .22 ammunition which, with the routine supplies issued to the Club, enabled the training to proceed rapidly at a time when the absence of .22 ammunition was only equalled by the scarcity of rifles. The Board maintained for as long as necessary a staff of 24 instructors under the supervision of Capt. Drew and the Assistant Secretary, who was seconded from his civil duties to deal with the enormous amount of clerical work. The attendance of Home Guards on these ranges totalled in all nearly 150,000 in addition to 1,900 on the revolver range and 7,600 with automatic weapons. Right up to the final stand-down, training continued intensively. As late as July 1944 a new 30-yds. full-bore range was erected near Stanmore to meet the increasing demand by men whose duties made long journeys difficult.

A *Home Guard Supplement* on the lines of the London Transport's Magazine, *Pennyfare*, was placed at the disposal of the Home Guard Group for the duration of the war from May 1940. The first number appeared entitled *The Home Guard, Supplement to Pennyfare*. It was edited by Mr. Alan Burton, employed in the Board's A.R.P. department. When Mr. Burton left in July of the following year

the editorship was taken over by Capt. H. G. R. Stevenson, of the A.R.P. department, who was also Group Gas and P.A.D. Officer.

The 'Journal', as it was popularly called, appeared monthly until the December edition in 1944. Some 12,000 copies were distributed each month via battalions, companies and platoons. Paper shortage reduced it to a four-page octavo folder for most of its run, but it nevertheless managed to carry news of all the battalions. Most editions had pictures of the Home Guard at work and at play. In addition, special items were included, such as the birthday parades, inspections by high ranking officers, etc.

The Journal published a Christmas Card each year, using an appropriate regimental motif ; these were very popular with all ranks. Officers Commanding Battalions, and others, wrote special articles from time to time. The Journal proved to be a popular link between all ranks, and copies found their way to many parts of the world.

As the war progressed, the use of vehicles for training became progressively more difficult and the generous allocation made by the Board in the early years could not be continued. Exercise Gadfly provided a major departure from these restrictions when the Regional Transport Commissioner authorised the use of 65 buses for a great London exercise.

The Group Medical Adviser, Lieut. Col. G. Morgan Evans, presented a Challenge Cup to the Unit in 1944. Known as the Morgan Evans Cup, this was awarded to the best battalion first-aid team and included stretcher drill, first aid in the field and general turn-out. The first contest, held at the South Training Camp in February 1944, resulted in a satisfactory win for the 44th Batt. although the general standard throughout was commented upon most favourably by the Adjudicator, Lieut. Col. Keogh, F Sector Medical Adviser.

In the Birthday Honours of 1944 the Unit received its highest honour when the leadership, tenacity and hard work of Col. Brook gained recognition by his appointment as a Commander of the Order of the British Empire. In addition to the several honours and awards in the Civil List to members of London Transport who were in their Home Guard, the following received official recognition for their services in the force :

Lieut. Col. H. K. Cleary	O.B.E.
Lieut. Col. J. B. Woodward	O.B.E.
Sgt. S. W. Chambers	B.E.M.
Lieut. A. J. Holloway	
	Commendation by G.O.C. in London District Orders
2nd Lt. A. J. Breadmore	do.
C.S.M. G. E. Dunn, H.L.I.	
(P.S.I. to the 60th Batt.)	do.
Cpl. G. W. McCarty	do.
Pte. W. H. Hewitt (decd.)	do.

GENERAL SIR CHARLES LLOYD,
K.C.B., D.S.O., M.C.

In addition 105 officers and other ranks were awarded Certificates of Merit. Their names are given at the end of their respective battalion chapters.

One of the last important duties undertaken by the London Transport's Unit was on November 11, 1944, when men of the 43rd Batt. joined with No. 1 Coy. of the 1st London (Westminster) Batt. to mount guard over the Unknown Warrior's Tomb in Westminster Abbey. This was the fourth occasion in which members of the London Transport's Home Guard had participated in this guard mounting. In 1941 the 42nd Batt. were concerned, but as a result of the re-organisation the honour was transferred to the 43rd Batt. for the remaining three years. A feature of mounting this guard was the complete absence of any verbal orders, all movements being controlled by a tap of the stick carried by the Guards Sgt. Major. On this occasion Col. Brook inspected the guard outside Westminster Abbey.

Amongst the enormous crowd at the Stand Down parade in Hyde Park on December 3, 1944, attended by the King, the Queen and both Princesses, were many London Transport Home Guards and their families intent on seeing not only the seven London Transport contingents of two officers and 18 other ranks each, but also the

L.P.T.B. Unit Military Band and the Pipe Band of the 41st Batt. which led the Scottish Command contingent. This was the only Pipe Band in the march and received a great welcome from the crowds. They also had the distinction of being particularly selected by the newsreel cameramen traversing the column.

Thus did the Home Guard stand down, still keen and still disappointed that they had not 'seen the whites of their eyes'.

Few people realised the tremendous task which had faced the pioneers of the London Transport Unit and the difficulties which were always present in adequately training a shift-workers' army.

London Transport's area covered some 2,000 square miles. Its properties included 82 bus garages, 31 tram and trolleybus depots, 181 railway stations, three generating stations, five overhaul works and a large number of substations. Had the necessity arisen, all would have been defended. During the life of the Home Guard not one case of sabotage occurred. Over and above all this, some 8,000 of London Transport's Home Guard stood ready to fight for the general defence of London as distinct from London Transport's properties. Each sub-unit fitted into the plan of defence and each could and would have played its part till the last. The 12,695 officers and men still in the Unit at the end can always be justly proud of their record. In all, over 30,000 men passed through the London Transport Unit, a total of which London Transport can always feel very proud.

4 Fighting the Bombs

REFERENCES to acts of bravery and devotion to duty by Home Guards must inevitably be incomplete ; only the men mentioned in the citations really know how much remains untold. The British gift for understatement is as apparent in what the Home Guard made known as in everything else—and many a deed of outstanding gallantry was never mentioned at all . . .

On September 18, 1940, Volunteer R. J. Elson, A Coy., 43rd Batt., a bus conductor at Willesden Garage, was detailed to help a patrol of the local Home Guard in tracing someone who flashed a torch during a raid. While the search was going on a bomb fell in an adjacent house. Elson immediately ran into the ruins and at great personal risk rescued a baby and then ran back again to save the mother, who was pinned by debris. He gave first-aid treatment to both of them and then went with them to hospital. The Guard Commander sent two other members of the Guard, who helped the Civil Defence to rescue a man who was buried except for one hand. Volunteer Elson was awarded the Home Guard Certificate of Merit.

On September 28, 1940, Volunteer J. Reynolds, 45th Batt., had reached Isleworth on his way home from guard duty at Hounslow Trolleybus Depot when incendiaries began to fall round a school. Water was not available, so Reynolds somehow scooped the bombs up one by one in his steel helmet and carried them from the building into the roadway. He did not report injury ; his helmet was ruined. On the same night more incendiaries dropped near petrol pumps at Hounslow Garage, and this time it was Volunteer J. Stanton who used his steel

NORTHOVER PRACTICE—SOUTH TRAINING CAMP

helmet to take the bombs away. Both men were awarded the Certificate of Merit.

Then there is Volunteer A. J. Breadmore, a trolleybus driver, No. 3 Platoon, 46th Batt. He was on service on October 14, 1940, when a bomb demolished a house in front of him. The house caught fire, but Breadmore forced his way in and rescued several people before proceeding on service. Six nights later Breadmore got another chance—he was at Finchley Depot when four high explosive bombs fell quite close. He was told that a man was buried in a shattered house, but that it was dangerous to go near because a gas main had broken. Breadmore ignored the risk, forced his way into the debris and found an elderly man trapped in fallen masonry. He called to Cpl. Lamb of his platoon to help and the man was rescued, although a great deal of water from a broken pipe poured on them all the time. Volunteer Breadmore was commended in Home Guard London District Orders.

Pte. E. Price, Middle Row Bus Garage, 60th Batt., was one of the Home Guards who found time to be a warden as well. He had attended 34 incidents in all when, about four o'clock one morning he found a four-storey house had been almost demolished. The escape of gas was so great that breathing was very difficult. With another warden, Pte. Price entered the building and saved two women. They re-entered the building and brought out a third woman and were going in again when they all but collapsed and had to be brought out themselves for recovery in the open air. The Civil Defence authorities reported what had happened and Pte. Price was awarded the George Medal, Civil Division.

On November 7, 1940, Platoon Commander Cameron, Sgt. Major Sharp and Pte. Harmer, 46th Batt., went to an incident in North Finchley where a high explosive bomb had caused much damage and a fire. They were told that several girls were trapped in a shelter. Making their way to the back of the burning building they found the shelter and forced the door open, freeing eleven people including one elderly woman. The entire Guard was then turned out to help the N.F.S. Reporting the incident the Platoon Commander said, ' The response to my order was magnificent. I have not before witnessed such team spirit and courage. After two and a half hours of fire-fighting they returned to their guard room, cut, bruised and saturated, but still smiling and ready to carry on duty '.

Cpl. G. W. McCarty, 43rd Batt., a garage warden at Victoria Garage, was on duty when a delayed action bomb fell in the roadway and set fire to a number of electric cables in the crater. The bomb could be clearly seen, but McCarty went to it with a fire-extinguisher and played on the flames until he was satisfied that the fire was out. Cpl. McCarty was commended by the General Officer Commanding in Home Guard London District Orders.

On November 1, 1941, Warner Road Garage was hit and set on fire. Platoon Commander A. Sharman, 44th Batt., disregarding the flames and at great personal risk, entered the garage eight times and drove eight buses from the fire to the safety of the street. Platoon Commander Sharman was then due to report for his civil job as a tram driver and so, though smoke-grimed and wet, he reported and drove his tram as usual for eight hours. Platoon Commander Sharman later received the O.B.E. Civil Division.

Good sense, always a feature of the Home Guard rescue work, was noted again in March 1941 when Platoon Commander Essex, C Coy., 45th Batt., called out his guard when a woman and six children were buried in the debris of a house. They started to release the woman, pinned by a beam and a door, and while doing so found and released a baby. There were no tools and the Home Guard had to dig with their hands. Platoon Commander Essex saw that the rescue work presented special problems, realised the limitations of Home Guard rescue experience, and directed the efforts of his men into proper channels, thus greatly aiding the trained rescue squads.

One Home Guard, Volunteer F. Greenaway, 44th Batt., ran great risk on November 16, 1940, when an English bomber crashed in Kent and caught fire. In company with two civilians, he cut the pilot free from the blazing machine which might have exploded at any moment and then returned for an aircraftsman. The aircraft was destroyed. Volunteer Greenaway gained the Home Guard Certificate of Merit. Certificates of Merit also were awarded to Cpl. W. Golding and Pte. J. G. Wrigley, 42nd Batt., for assisting in rescue work when a bomb fell near the Streatham Hill Tram Depot. They heard cries for assistance coming from beneath a big heap of rubble and began to clear the bricks away. They were joined by the Civil Defence, and had to dig to a depth of nearly 5 ft. before the victim could be extricated. Pte. Wrigley returned to the depot and went out on service ignoring the fact that he had sprained an ankle.

Home Guard action to counter enemy attacks took many forms. The transfer of Home Guards to anti-aircraft batteries in 1943 did not at first apply to London Transport, but in September 1943 all battalions were asked to help. At first the Unit found response difficult because only men working settled civilian hours of employment could be fitted into teams always available at a settled time; youth and strength were essentials too. Nevertheless London Transport answered the call and some 250 men were transferred to Heavy and Z rocket batteries in all parts of London.

Anti-bomb work, however, started in the summer of 1941, when industrial establishments employing 500 people or more were invited to form their own voluntary bomb disposal units to reduce the loss of time in dealing with unexploded bombs. The Board formed squads at Chiswick and Acton works. In 1942 the Government decided that the War Office should take over these units. Many of the Acton men were already members of the 45th Batt., and those in the Chiswick squad were attached to the 43rd Batt. A call for volunteers resulted in the strength of these squads being doubled, and in February 1943 they were transferred to Royal Engineer Coys. for training and operations and remained with the Home Guard only for administration purposes. In addition to the Acton and Chiswick Units six men of No. 18 Platoon, Northfleet, 44th Batt., volunteered and qualified for bomb disposal duties with the 17th Kent Batt.

The extent to which these men were called upon by the R.E. Bomb Disposal Coys. varied considerably ; in the opinion of the men fortune favoured the 45th Batt. unit. A renewal of bombing in 1944 gave an opportunity for training to be put to the test. Lieut. Humphries received his first call from the 24th Coy. Bomb Disposal Unit, R.E., on February 26, a Sunday. After working all day he and his team had the satisfaction of finding and extricating two 50 kg. bombs in Kensington. On the following two Sundays the unit worked, largely without R.E. supervision, on building a caisson over a 1,800 kg. high explosive bomb at Sunbury and then, six days later, they completed an excavation at Twickenham and found and removed a 500 kg. armour-piercing bomb which was in 15 ft. of gravel and running water. Lieut. Humphries received a Certificate of Merit.

The 43rd Batt., Chiswick unit, led by Lieut. G. W. Mathews, were also busy. On March 5, after much digging and timbering-up, they reached a 500 kg. bomb at Brentford and on the following week-end relieved an R.E. squad which had been digging for a couple of weeks at Shepherds Bush for a 1,000 kg. high explosive bomb. On the latter incident, although four power pumps were used, the men worked continuously in water up to their knees.

Meanwhile, all battalions had answered the call for help to the Civil Defence, and Heavy Rescue Squads were formed and properly trained in all parts of London. Even when bombing lessened and stopped, training went on in all aspects of rescue work.

In March 1944 higher command decided that better anti-aircraft protection was needed at the Neasden generating station, and the greater part of the local Home Guard was formed into a light A.A. unit, which remained under Major R. G. Orsman and was designated 60th London A Troop, L.A.A. Capt. G. Grange was placed in charge of the Troop and all the original junior officers at Neasden became Troop relief officers. Eight pairs of twin L.A.A. Browning guns were set up in specially reinforced positions built at short notice by the Board. The Troop was under the operational command of the 26th A.A. Brigade and was allocated a P.S.I. from the Royal Artillery.

The infantry-turned-gunners worked hard at their new task, for Brownings call for high efficiency and mental alertness, especially in the recognition of all types of aircraft. The Company Commander's office became a plotting room connected by special telephone lines with the Gladstone Park Heavy A.A. Battery, where the A.T.S. girls worked

hard to speed the training of the Troop. Classes were held at all hours of most days each week at Neasden and were constantly visited by Capt. Martin, R.A. Teams for instruction were sent to the Dome Trainers at Mill Hill, Northolt, Hyde Park and, ultimately, to the coast for target practice ; all troops got the A.A. shoulder flashes for their uniform and were given more and more ' practice runs ' from Gladstone Park Battery. All ranks became very competent and remained extremely keen. The result was that in May 1944 they reached a standard of efficiency which brought high praise from the R.A. instructors.

On the night of June 15/16 an air raid alert was sounded before midnight and was still ' on ' at dawn. At 7.10 a.m. the 60th L.A.A. received the order ' Stand to ' ; it sent a big thrill through all ranks. In working clothes and steel helmets the men ran to the gun towers, climbed them and loaded the guns—the steady chant of the A.T.S. plotters meant something real at last. Many times that day the troop heard and answered the same call. Then came an order that A.A. fire against flying bombs would cease inside the London area ; nor was A.A. fire of any avail against the rockets. But the 60th L.A.A. had this satisfaction— they were the first and only complete unit of the London Transport Home Guard to be actually called to action stations.

Flying bombs and rockets yielded opportunities for London Transport Home Guard.

On June 23, 1944, Pte. K. Keeting, 42nd Batt., reached a shelter which had been hit and was joined there by Pte. G. S. Wilkin of the same battalion. There were cries for help and the two Home Guards began to clear away debris. Finally, after heavy concrete blocks had been removed, they found and released a man—L/Cpl. Poole of the 42nd Batt. Despite his serious injuries Poole was able to indicate that his wife and other women were still in the wreckage. Keeting and Wilkin worked untiringly with

the Civil Defence to try to save more lives and the remaining people were recovered ; they were dead. Pte. Wilkin and Keeting both received a Certificate of Merit.

During a fly-bomb attack on July 27, 1944, Pte. William Henry Hewitt, 41st Batt., was going to his Coy. H.Q. when a flying bomb was heard approaching. A queue of people waited at the bus stop and pedestrians were passing. Pte. Hewitt ran along the road shouting, ' This one is for us—take cover everybody '. People obeyed him without question and at once. A few seconds later the bomb fell in the roadway ; Pte. Hewitt was the only fatal casualty. His gallantry was commended by the General Officer Commanding in London District Home Guard Orders.

Considerable damage was done by a fly-bomb on June 25, 1944, to Flora Gardens Schools, which were used by the 43rd Batt. Sgt. F. W. Jowers and Ptes. Cheshire and W. C. Davis, B Coy., of this battalion, entered an adjoining house which was severely knocked about and rescued an elderly man from the debris.

The first call from the Civil Defence for assistance during the fly-bomb attacks was on the night of June 22, 1944, when the 60th Task Platoon was called to a large fire at Cricklewood to protect shop property and stocks and to help to control the crowds. From this date till the end of the war the Board's Home Guards were kept busy. In addition to normal rescue work the 44th Batt. provided a first-aid team every night in the Deptford area. It was controlled by Sgt. Burrows, who personally attended a very large number of casualties. The Battalion Commander, commending Sgt. Burrows, wrote, ' I have received details of nearly 100 individual instances where you have given first aid, not only to the Home Guard, but to the public. The reputation of your section stands so high that people have been sent to you for treatment from quite a distance. In addition, you have been manning a light rescue vehicle nightly during the same period and I understand that during this time you have put in no fewer than 1,836 hours of duty'.

Pte. Pew, Old Kent Road Platoon, 44th Batt., also did excellent work. He had nearly 100 hours of duty at eight different fly-bomb incidents in Brockley, Nunhead, Peckham, Catford and Forest Hill, and on one occasion worked from 5.0 a.m. till 11.15 p.m. without a break. In the afternoon of July 12, 1944, a bomb fell in residential property in Willesden Green. All available men in the 60th Batt. headquarters were mustered and went to the scene. Colour-Sgt. R. C. Wells was in the party which rescued a two-year-old child after two hours of constant digging. The mother, lying across the child, had saved its life and given her own.

Following are extracts from the 44th and 41st Batt. records : ' During the fly-bomb period Elmers End Garage received a direct hit and was destroyed. The Guard Room was demolished and ten people were killed including two members of the platoon. Sgt. Cunningham was killed while roof spotting and the last thing he did was ring the alarm bell. Lieut. Jeffrey, M.M., Platoon Commander, was buried in debris but was not badly hurt. The Platoon Officer, Lieut. Hyde, led members of the platoon throughout the night under the direction of the Adjutant, and all acquitted themselves with the greatest credit. Bexley, Nunhead and Camberwell tram and bus garages were all damaged, while they were in the 44th Batt. area. There were no serious casualties, but in every instance the platoons mustered and rendered all possible help. The guard at Nunhead did particularly good work and the Commander. Cpl. Smithers, was awarded a Certificate of Merit. Once a 500 lb. bomb went through battalion headquarters into the bus station below. It did not explode, but later, when exploded by a bomb disposal squad, considerable damage was done. Battalion headquarters, by that time, had been evacuated to Chief Office.'

The 41st Batt. rendered assistance at the following fly-bomb incidents in July : ' On July 18 H.Q., A and E Coys. supplied detachments for rescue work and police duties at four incidents. A Coy. supplied further detachments on the 23rd for police duties, on the 27th for debris clearance, and on the 29th for anti-looting patrols. D Coy. attended incidents on London Transport property on the 23rd and 30th.' Thus very much good work is compressed into little space.

On July 24 the 60th Task Platoon was called at 5.0 a.m. to a fly-bomb incident in poor property in Kilburn. Major Eyres and Lieut. Seymour led the contingent, but had to be withdrawn to prepare for their civilian duties. They had only just returned when there was a further urgent call from this incident. Lieut. Col. Woodward raised a team which included an ex-member of the battalion Pte. Fowler, on leave from the Royal Marines, who worked splendidly though due to return from leave in a few hours. This incident was a bad one and digging went on for five and a half hours. A few hours later units of the American Army came to relieve the 60th team, which received high praise from the Willesden Civil Defence authorities.

Another incident in the same borough occurred about noon on August 21. Despite the difficulty of contacting men at this time a team was raised and it worked continuously for five hours. recovering seven victims, of whom only one was alive. Later the battalion was asked to provide further assistance at this incident and a fresh team of one officer and ten men worked until 2.0 a.m. Two more victims were recovered, both dead. Lieut. Col. Woodward reported, ' It is difficult to name any outstanding acts, as everyone, without exception, worked untiringly and on this occasion were called upon to witness most unfortunate things which were new to the majority of the Home Guard present.' That sentence is true of much Home Guard work during the bombing from one end of the Board's area to the other end.

Here is an extract from a report by the 60th Batt. submitted to London District Headquarters : 'A V.1 bomb fell near the 60th H.Q. at Shoot-up-Hill on Tuesday, August 15. In doing so it sucked out the front of a house on the opposite side of the road and caused a side wall to bulge. This resulted in the second floor hanging at a dangerous angle and furniture falling into the front garden. The lady on this floor had the presence of mind, when rolling down the floor with the furniture, to seize the edge of the carpet ; she came to a stop hanging over the edge of the floor. She was saved by Lieut. A. J. Holloway and C.S.M. G. E. Durr, Highland Light Infantry, P.S.I. of the battalion. To accomplish the rescue it was necessary to make a human chain across the sloping, broken floor, and in this Lieut. Holloway and C.S.M. Durr were prominent links. A rope was passed down this human chain and made fast to the lady after which it was possible for an extending ladder to be held erect from the garden below by members of the N.F.S. and the Home Guard.' Lieut. Holloway and C.S.M. Durr both received commendations in London District Orders.

5 The Bands

THE UNIT BAND

THROUGH the ages martial music has played a prominent part in the life of British regiments, and in the Home Guard it was not surprising that many old soldiers remarked on its absence.

Many regular bands came to their assistance, but this was not enough. The Home Guard wanted a band of their own, and the War Office would not pay for what might appear a luxury.

Instruments were at a premium and complete sets almost unobtainable, but musicians were available in the ranks, though often very scattered.

The search for secondhand instruments began in earnest. From Boosey & Hawkes to the smallest side road dealers ex-regular bandsmen brought treasured instruments. The talk after parades, amongst a select few, turned to euphoniums, basses, lips, more practice, clarinets, pitch, bassoons, drums—drums—drums. The Home Guard did not intend to be mute.

A Coy. of the 43rd Batt. were amongst the first groups striving to form battalion bands. Lord Ashfield realised at once that bands could not be set up without funds, and Col. Brook's suggestion that this embryo should be made into the L.P.T.B. Unit Home Guard Band was accepted. Led by the Chairman, the Officers of the Board generously subscribed to make it an accomplished fact From five men in February 1941 the band grew to 25 by April, and in May the band made their first appearance, complete with their own instruments, at the Anniversary Parade at Osterley.

They appeared again the next day for a

THE UNIT MILITARY BAND

parade of A Coy. of the 43rd Batt. at Cricklewood.

London Transport's peace-time Military Band, the T.O.T. Band, helped by lending music, stands and drums, and later tympanis for concert work. A few of its members played regularly with the Home Guard.

During the summer the band attended parades of the 41st, 43rd, 44th and 46th Batts., besides entertaining the staff at lunch on the forecourt of Cricklewood Garage and Stonebridge Depot. Their progress was such that, by October, they were looking for public engagements.

On October 26, 1941, they had their first audition at the Gaumont State Cinema, Kilburn, and were successful. This was no mean achievement for a set of musicians most of whom had not seen each other before, and many of whom had picked up their instruments again after a lapse of many years. Great credit was due to their leader, Lieut. Monk, and they were fortunate in the number of ex-Regular Army bandsmen in their midst. Against this, practices, essential to any band worth hearing, were a permanent worry. With the exception of three or four men, every member was a shift worker, not all on the same shift. Col. Brook's efforts for the band throughout its life solved many problems, but only by constant applications for change of shifts and

rest days. More important engagements were helped by the management by granting leave but, such is the nature of public transport life, that this was by no means easy.

The band made its first public appearance at the State Cinema, Kilburn, on November 21, 1941, and followed this by a tour of other large Gaumont cinemas. Throughout this time the band was led by Lieut. Monk, an ex-Regular bandsman trained at Kneller Hall. He knew and understood musical temperament and the peculiarities of transport shift work, being a bus conductor himself. His happy disposition and conscientious leadership made the band what it was. From an unknown group of musicians with a mixed selection of instruments he made a band, which in ten months played Tchaikowsky's Overture '1812' before a packed house at the Orpheum, Golders Green. Lord Ashfield attended this special Sunday concert on March 8, 1942.

Two weeks later the band again appeared in public when, in 'Warships Week' they played at Chiswick Empire amongst such distinguished musicians as Albert Sandler and Mark Hambourg.

During 1942 they played at many battalion marches and church parades. They entertained the Army Kinema Service at Wembley and led Wembley Unit of the R.A.O.C. on church parade in June. The

Acton works staff heard them twice when they played in the canteen at lunch.

On August 18 they played to the staff in Chiswick works canteen. After this performance their President, Lieut. Col. Woodward, presented Lieut. Monk with a gold wrist watch, subscribed by members of the band. Two days later Lieut. Monk left to join the Regular Army. The loss of their leader was a serious blow to the band and many weeks passed before a successor was appointed. Capt. E. J. Bates, Quartermaster to the 46th Batt., and another Kneller Hall musician became Musical Director in October, 1942, and under his leadership the band undertook more classical work, which resulted in their broadcasting in the 'Listen to the Band' programme on May 30, 1943. This was followed by a series of engagements for the Holidays-at-Home programmes in the public parks of North-West London.

Up to this time they retained the original mixed instruments of their early days. In July 1943 the Board generously met the cost of replacement with low pitch instruments.

In June of this year the band left London for the first time to play in the Holidays-at-Home programme at Rochester Castle, Kent. In the following August they played twice in the Municipal Bandstand at Westcliff-on-Sea.

In addition to their regimental engagements with the battalions, they were engaged at Rochester Castle again on two occasions in 1944. They had the privilege of being one of the few bands ever to play at Westcliff on three separate week-ends in one season, thus visiting the resort four times in 12 months, getting a great welcome on each occasion.

The anniversary Unit Parades always found the band at their best and at full strength, which, from early 1943, was 35.

On December 3, 1944, the King took the salute of the Home Guard in Hyde Park when they marched through London at their stand down. The L.P.T.B. Unit Home Guard Band was included in this, the Home Guard's finest march.

As the large crowds cheered them along the route for the last time, they played themselves out on the top of their form.

THE CORPS OF DRUMS

A Corps of Drums and Bugles, raised by Lieut. Col. Woodward in August 1941 was placed under the command of Drum Major P. C. Brown, of Cricklewood Bus Garage. The military band had by this time received permission from Winchester to play the

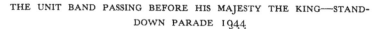

THE UNIT BAND PASSING BEFORE HIS MAJESTY THE KING—STAND-
DOWN PARADE 1944

AT THE GAUMONT STATE CINEMA

regimental bugle march of the King's Royal Rifle Corps on all appropriate occasions. The Corps of Drums was massed with the military band on most occasions when this march was played. These included several appearances on London stages in addition to frequent March Pasts of battalions.

In October 1942 Drum Major Brown relinquished his position and from then on the corps was led by Drum Major Elles of Victoria Garage. The strength increased slightly and was maintained at 21 until the stand down. This unit provided buglers on many occasions for the L.P.T.B. and other battalions at the funeral services of Home Guards. They also attended at Fulham and Finchley during the 'Salute the Soldier' week.

The 46th Battalion always took a keen interest in the corps of drums and presented them with a number of bugles. One of their most memorable parades was at Hedgerley in 1943 when they accompanied the 60th Batt. at one of the week-end camps. Besides playing the battalion in and out of camp, the buglers provided all calls throughout the week-end and beat Retreat before leaving the camp on Sunday evening.

After playing at the stand down parades of the 46th and 60th Batts., the corps reluctantly met at Stonebridge Trolleybus Depot on December 11, 1944 to stand down, but this was not, as everyone reasonably supposed, their last appearance.

On June 17, 1945, the Middlesex Civil Defence held a County stand down parade in Wembley Stadium. As a mark of appreciation for the assistance given to the Middlesex Civil Defence by the Home Guard, the 12th Middlesex Batt. and the 60th London L.P.T.B. Batt. Home Guard were invited to send contingents. The Corps of Drums was hastily called by letter and wire, while drums and bugles were assembled and examined.

Little time was available for practice except on the actual morning of the parade, yet they made a brave show as they played the Home Guard from Wembley Park to the Stadium. They gave the general salute in the Stadium with the massed bugle bands of all three branches of the pre-service Units. After a tiring day the Corps of Drums played the Home Guard away from the Stadium.

This was a fitting finale of a very keen team whom so many will always remember when they hear the stirring bugle refrain of *The Wild Hunt* by Lutznow.

43RD BATT. MILITARY BAND

The 43rd Batt. brass band was enrolled in 1942. The Commanding Officer had discussed the formation of a band within the battalion and learnt that a member of the Shepherds Bush garage platoon was also a member of the Hammersmith Borough Silver Prize Band, conducted by Mr. A. E. Ashcroft. The Secretary, Mr. F. W. Dickenson, arranged an audition and so impressed the 43rd Batt. C.O. that after a brief round-table talk it was agreed the band should be enrolled at once. Thus the 43rd Batt. military band came into being. At this time there were not 20 regular musicians, but the efforts of Sgt. Dickenson attracted other bandsmen. In a few months the strength had reached 30.

As a musical director Lieut. A. E. Ashcroft was outstanding. The band was very fortunate in having the enthusiastic leadership of such an accomplished musician, who had coached bands for successes at the Crystal Palace Band Festival. Here was no mere ' stick wagger ' who was content with ' good results '. A strict disciplinarian, Lieut. Ashcroft did not hesitate to deal suitably with men for over-blowing or failing to remember a correction at a previous practice.

He had an ear which could tell whether or not a flageolet was playing in a full orchestra. After a few practices, the band, now wearing khaki, was doing its work in first-rate style. Within a few months the standard of playing rose considerably and the band fulfilled many engagements in London parks during 1943.

They reached their peak when, on Sunday, October 17, 1943, they broadcast in the ' Listen to the Band ' programme.

The record would be incomplete without

THE ORPHEUM, GOLDERS GREEN

reference to Mrs. Dickenson, who carried on the duty of Band Secretary after Sgt. Dickenson was called to the Regular Army.

The ' Holidays-at-Home ' season of 1944 gave the band opportunities to play to the public at more than 40 performances, and during this year they again broadcast.

41st BATT. PIPE BAND

In 1942 the 41st Batt. decided that they should have a battalion band, but, unlike their colleagues, preferred a pipe band, which was formed by Major P. Beckers and Sgt. G. Patterson, an ex-piper of the London Irish Rifles.

Enquiries in the battalion produced a number of musicians but few trained pipers and drummers. Whilst this would have deterred most units, it seemed to inspire the 41st to set about the difficult task of training Englishmen, Scotsmen and Irishmen to play pipes which many of them had never handled before.

The drumming, which in this type of band is not at all easy, was undertaken on similar lines ; Pte. G. Skeggs assisted. Inspector Wright, of the trolleybuses, became Drum Major, a duty he performed with skill. After several months' training the band made its

CORPS OF DRUMS

C

first appearance on August 15, 1943, when the battalion marched from Loxford Hall to Manor Park for a Sunday morning exercise.

From then onwards the band paraded probably more often than any other band in the Unit and were to be seen practically every Sunday playing either a battalion or a company to and from training areas. They attended the Group Parade in Hyde Park in 1944, and played the 41st Batt. past the Saluting Base. In addition to their marching their reels were a popular feature of battalion and company dances.

The pipe band attended at the 60th Batt. stand down parade and were also lent to the 4th Essex Batt. for a ceremonial parade. They provided the music at the parades of the West Ham Old Contemptibles in 1943 and 1944, and headed the march of these old warriors to their Remembrance Service at St. John's Church.

Their greatest honour was London District's request for them to lead the Scottish contingent in the great stand down march past before the King in December 1944. Of the many bands on parade they received the greatest applause from the crowds lining the route. The newsreel cameramen selected particularly the 41st Pipers in their 'shots' of the march.

Major P. Beckers remained Band President throughout the life of the band. The appointment of Sgt. G. Patterson as Pipe Major was justly deserved. The outstanding success of this band was largely due to his efforts and attention to training.

The band normally paraded ten pipers, four side drums and a base drum, but a system of training was introduced which resulted in a small but steady intake of trainees. At the time of the stand down the band was 25 strong, including those under instruction. These men were drawn mostly from the staff of the Central Buses, but also included the Trolleybus and Railway Departments.

Their last duty with the battalion was the stand down at Loxford Hall on Nov. 19, 1944,

but they were at the head of the Scottish contingent marching through London when the wail of their pipes receded into the past.

44TH BATT. MILITARY BAND

Shortly after the 44th Batt. was formed it had the good fortune to receive an offer from Mr. J. Clifton, J.P., Secretary of the London Tram and Trolleybus Central Sports Association, of the loan of a set of silver band instruments which had formerly been used by the band of that association.

This was gratefully accepted and the search for musicians began. Some were already in the battalion, but the majority were recruited from non-Board employees. The first Bandmaster was Sgt. Burke, who studied music under Gustav Holst, but his civil duties would not permit him to devote the amount of time to the band which he would have wished, and Lieut. Rawlings (nominal Assistant Adjutant), with wide experience of band work, succeeded him and remained Bandmaster until the battalion was disbanded.

The band played on route marches and church parades, and also in church at the services, and was massed with the L.P.T.B. bands for the reviews in Hyde Park in 1943 and 1944. It also played at social functions, as did the dance band section of it, and filled several engagements with public bodies on the occasion of savings drives, etc.

Instruments were returned to the association when the battalion stood down.

41ST BATTALION PIPE BAND

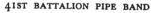

6 The 41st Battalion

THE First Battalion, predecessors of the 41st, were recruited from the London Transport railwaymen and from the Civil Engineer's Department. Mr. R. F. Morkill (Signal Engineer's Department), became organiser for the battalion in May 1940 and the deputy organiser, Mr. T. H. Peerless (Building Department), was appointed Battalion Commander in June 1940, and later gazetted Lieutenant Colonel. Mr. Morkill continued his association with the battalion until February 1941, when he was seconded to Group Headquarters with the rank of Major.

The Adjutant (unpaid) was Mr. D. S. Prosser, and Mr. W. C. Leany was Quartermaster. During the first few months Mr. W. A. Dobson acted as 2 i/c Batt., in addition to commanding A Coy.

Five companies formed the original battalion. The organisation which covered a considerable area, including miles of railway track, was :

A Company
O.C. : W. A. Dobson
Platoon Commanders : Messrs. Sisson and Munro

B Company
O.C. : E. A. F. Johnston
Platoon Commanders : Messrs. Clark, Mahoney, Bond and McLeod

C Company
O.C. : J. Field
Platoon Commanders : Messrs. Havers and Cowan

D Company
O.C. : J. Tyndale
Platoon Commanders : Messrs. Morris and Menzies

E Company
O.C. : E. McCracken
Platoon Commanders : Messrs. Wickham, Edrich and Heavens

In the absence of official warrant ranks at this time the following were given acting rank :

R.Q.M.S. : C. Cruse
C.S.M., A Coy. : B. S. Taylor
C.S.M., B Coy. : E. G. Brown
C.S.M., C Coy. : F. W. Potter
C.S.M., D Coy. : J. Fletcher
C.S.M., E Coy. : E. W. Payne
C.Q.M.S., A Coy. : S. V. Pereira
C.Q.M.S., B Coy. : H. H. Martin
C.Q.M.S., C Coy. : R. D. Davies
C.Q.M.S., D Coy. : T. E. Evans
C.Q.M.S., E Coy. : C. Hart

By the end of 1940 the organisation carried 20 platoons and with authorisation of commissions to the Home Guard on February 1, 1941, the following were the first company and platoon commanders to receive official rank :

Major T. S. Munro	A Coy.
Major E. W. Clark	B Coy.
Major J. Field	C Coy.
Major J. A. G. Tyndale	D Coy.
Major E. McCracken	E Coy.
Lieut. J. B. Dalton	No. 1 Plat., A Coy.
Lieut. W. F. Challis	No. 2 Plat., A Coy.
Lieut. G. L. S. Webster	No. 3 Plat., A Coy.
Lieut. L. J. Ellis	No. 4 Plat., A Coy.
Lieut. A. V. Bond	No. 5 Plat., B Coy.
Lieut. R. H. Budgen	No. 6 Plat., B Coy.
Lieut. W. J. Mahoney	No. 7 Plat., B Coy.
Lieut. G. H. Crowfoot	No. 8 Plat., B Coy.
Lieut. A. J. Holloway	No. 9 Plat., C Coy.
Lieut. F. W. Potter	No. 10 Plat., C Coy.
Lieut. J. W. D. Kelly	No. 11 Plat., C Coy.
Lieut. H. A. Wickham	No. 12 Plat., C Coy.
Lieut. A. V. Elliott	No. 13 Plat., D Coy.
Lieut. R. Collins	No. 14 Plat., D Coy.
Lieut. D. Menzies	No. 15 Plat., D Coy.
Lieut. J. H. Glover	No. 16 Plat., D Coy.
Lieut. H. M. Earl	No. 17 Plat., E Coy.

Lieut. W. Woodhouse   No. 18 Plat., E Coy.
Lieut. E. W. Payne   No. 19 Plat., E Coy.
Lieut. E. Long   No. 20 Plat., E Coy.

The following B.H.Q. Officers were also commissioned :

Lieut. R. W. Farrant   Batt. Signals Officer
Lieut. B. W. Pannel   Batt. Intell. Officer
Lieut. C. W. F. Randall   Assist. Adj. & Q.M.

Six months later the Battalion Medical Officer, Major V. B. Green-Armitage was commissioned.

Mr. Johnston relinquished command of B Coy. on his transfer to the Ministry of Aircraft Production, and was succeeded by Mr. E. W. Clark. Mr. Dobson also resigned owing to pressure of work and the command of A Coy. was taken over by Mr. T. S. Munro. The first H.Q. was in the lower ground floor of Baker Street station offices, but moved to another part of the building when hit by a bomb in January 1941. They moved to

Baker Street Bakerloo after being hit again in May 1941, and remained for the next 14 months. The splendid work of the A and Q staffs on both these occasions was instrumental in avoiding what might easily have been complete disorganisation.

In March 1941 battalions were given county names, and the 1st Batt. became the 41st County of London L.P.T.B. Batt. Commissions had been granted during the previous month. Capt. D. S. Prosser was seconded to the M.A.P. in October 1941, and found it impossible to continue his adjutant's duties. The battalion, therefore, lost a most valuable and loyal officer. Capt. W. C. Leaney took over the adjutant's duties and became A and Q Officer, his performance of this double task continuing for nine months until the appointment of Regular Officers.

During 194 exercises had for their main lesson the defence of a section of the perma-

LIEUTENANT-COLONEL T. H. P. PEERLESS WITH SENIOR OFFICERS
OF THE BATTALION

nent way, and sometimes outlying platoons were tested in open country. D Coy. records show a number of such 'battles' ranging from one platoon to several battalions. One of them exemplifies the team work between the Home Guard and other branches of the military and civil services.

On September 14, 1941, the 41st Batt., less D Coy., attacked Chalfont and Latimer Stations. D Coy., under Major J. A. G. Tyndale, together with the local Home Guard, defended the area. During the exercise aircraft repeatedly performed dummy dive-bombing runs over the defenders' lines. Umpires busied themselves by starting 'fires'. The A.R.P. carried out their part, calling fire-fighting units to every incident and even labelling civilian 'casualties' from the bombing and sending them to A.R.P. and Home Guard First Aid Posts. The police and Home Guard jointly treated all traffic as 'suspect' and checked registration cards and respirators at nine road barriers. During gas alerts the police and wardens again played a prominent part and asked civilians to put their masks on and take cover.

A few weeks later, on October 19, the battalion organised an exercise in which B, D and part of E Coy. were 'paratroops', the remainder of the battalion being detailed to deal with them. The open country selected lies midway between Berkhamsted and Rickmansworth. The 'enemy' marched out of Chesham to Leyhill Common and then split its attack, D and half of E Coy. attacking the village of Flaunden from the north and west, with B Coy. moving through woods, with Sarrat as their objective.

To reach this, B Coy. were instructed to hide in woods south of Flaunden until the northern attack had drawn off some of the defenders. The plan worked, but was helped by reserves from Sarrat losing their way and racing into the peaceful village of Chenies some way to the south and outside the scene of the exercise.

Meanwhile a fierce battle was raging round Flaunden, which is particularly interesting, as a special note in the exercise orders reads : 'Opponents must not close within ten yards of each other.' A truce for lunch resulted in a raid by both sides on the one 'local' in the village and a certain amount of confusion in putting the forces into their original positions after lunch.

Shortly before the exercise started it was learnt that the Herts Home Guard also had an exercise at right angles over the same area. Both exercises continued happily and without difficulty. By such experiences the Home Guard learnt its lessons. The 41st continued to stage exercises wherever possible over strange ground and preferably in the dark.

The reorganisation of London Transport's Unit on November 1, 1941, resulted in their taking over the north-eastern area of London. This caused a big changeover of troops. Many platoons in the north-east were transferred to other battalions and all London Transport battalions in this area were taken over, mainly by the 43rd and 46th Batts. With the exception of two Platoon Commanders the battalion lost the whole of its original Company Officers. Of the new officers transferred into the battalion the following were appointed to senior commands: Major T. T. Shephard, Second-in-Command, Battalion ; Major S. W. Edis, O.C., A Coy. ; Major F. R. Gessey, O.C., B Coy. ; Major T. W. King, O.C., C Coy. ; Major A. E. Hill, O.C., D Coy. ; Major J. Cross, O.C., E Coy. ; and Major P. Beckers, O.C., F Coy.

The organisation of the newly formed battalion was as follows :

A Company
No. 1 Platoon—Hackney (Trolleybus)
No. 2 Platoon—Hackney (Bus)
No. 3 Platoon—Dalston (Bus)
No. 4 Platoon—Clay Hall (Bus)
B Company
No. 5 Platoon—Bow (Trolleybus)
No. 6 Platoon—Poplar (Trolleybus)
No. 7 Platoon—Whitechapel (Railways)
No. 8 Platoon—Athol St. (Bus)

C Company

No. 9 Platoon—Leyton (Trolleybus)
No. 10 Platoon—Walthamstow (Trolleybus)
No. 11 Platoon—Leyton (Bus)
No. 12 Platoon—Loughton (Bus)
No. 13 Platoon—Epping (Bus)

D Company

No. 14 Platoon—Forest Gate (Bus)
No. 15 Platoon—Upton Park (Bus)
No. 16 Platoon—West Ham (Trolleybus)

E Company

No. 17 Platoon—Barking (Bus)
No. 18 Platoon—Seven Kings (Bus)
No. 19 Platoon—Ilford (Trolleybus)

F Company

No. 20 Platoon—Hornchurch (Bus)
No. 21 Platoon—Romford (Bus)
No. 22 Platoon—Grays (Bus)

No. 13 Platoon was transferred almost at once to F Coy. and the strength of the battalion at this stage was 55 officers and 2,227 other ranks.

The formation of the additional Company was necessary to cover country area platoons received from the 43rd Batt.

R.S.M. G. Norman was confirmed in his appointment on May 1, 1942, and he held the position until the stand down.

On June 29, 1942, 2nd Lt. J. H. Boreham, Royal Fusiliers, was appointed Quartermaster and soon after received his Captaincy. Two weeks later Capt. J. D. Canning, H.A.C., joined the battalion as adjutant. In October 1942 Major T. W. King relinquished his command of C Coy. and transferred to the 46th Batt. He was succeeded by Lieut. J. Brady, who was promoted to Major.

In February 1943 a H.Q. Company was formed by Major T. T. Shephard, Battalion 2 i/c, the command being later given to Major T. Beckers. F Coy. was taken over by Capt. Price, originally 2 i/c of that company. Lieut. C. Chenery received his Captaincy and became 2 i/c, subsequently taking command of the company in the rank of Major when Major Price resigned on March 4, 1944. Major F. R. Gessey, M.M., resigned his appointment on October 14, 1942, and accepted the position of Battalion P.A.D. Officer.

Capt. H. G. Cruse, 2 i/c D Coy., was promoted Major and transferred to command B Coy. The vacancy thus created was filled by the promotion of C.S.M. H. T. M. Scarborough.

In October 1943 the battalion received a severe blow when Major Brady, M.C., was accidentally killed when going to Home Guard duty at Loughton. He joined the battalion at the re-organisation as Platoon Commander, Loughton, and received rapid promotion because of his hard work and good leadership. Major Brady was one of the most popular and valuable officers in the battalion. His place was filled by the promotion of Capt. H. T. M. Scarborough, who was at that time 2 i/c D Coy. On October 1,

1943, Capt. J. F. Stitfall was appointed W.T.O. and later combined these duties with that of 2 i/c H.Q. Coy.

The operational role of the battalion was at first similar to other utility units. Their mobility resulted in the north-east sub-district detailing all the 41st general service troops, less F Coy., to be held in reserve as a mobile counter-attack force for use anywhere in the north-east area. The static forces for the defence of London Transport property came under the command of local battalions for operations, while F Coy., situated in the London Transport country area, were attached to local battalions in action.

Platoon headquarters were in garages and depots, where guard rooms had been built by London Transport, while battalion and company headquarters were mostly in requisitioned property. Lieut. Col. Peerless was fortunate in his last selection of a headquarters, and on July 27, 1942, took over Loxford Hall, Ilford, a large house with grounds. The size of both house and grounds lent itself to adaptation for all branches of training. A' Coy. headquarters was in a club in Mare Street, Hackney,

and included a large lecture hall.

B Coy. requisitioned a house at Devon Wharf, Poplar, and C Coy. obtained the British Legion headquarters in Hoe Street, Walthamstow, which also included a training hut. D Coy., based on West Ham Trolleybus Depot, secured St. Stephen's Hall, Green Street, Forest Gate, for training until at first damaged, then finally demolished, by fly-bombs. E Coy. were based on Loxford Hall, and F Coy. in a double-fronted shop at Iona Road, Hornchurch.

The training of the battalion was speeded by the accessibility of Rainham and Purfleet ranges, which offered facilities for rifle, Spigot, Northover and Smith gun-firing, in addition to bomb-throwing. The battalion also made full use of various Home Guard training schools, including Burwash Field-craft School, Hendon Physical Training G.H.Q. School, Denbies (Dorking) and the South-Eastern Army Weapon Training School.

During winter months indoor training was given largely by films, A, C and D Coys. training quarters being used in rotation, usually twice a week. The real assistance

given to the Home Guard during their winter training by the Army Kinema Unit cannot be too strongly emphasised.

During the special officers' training at Loxford Hall, Major T. T. Shephard, Batt. 2 i/c, gave monthly T.E.W.T.s on battle procedure which produced intelligent discussions and also gave selected officers an opportunity to show their prowess. Field training continued at all times while ceremonial parades were occasionally held at both company and battalion level. An example of the way in which ceremonial and training were combined is shown by the record of C Coy., whose parade on April 19, 1942, for inspection by the Battalion Commander was followed by the company splitting up into sub-units to demonstrate their many forms of training.

A few weeks later, on May 31, the battalion attended the Group parade before Brigadier Whitehead, C.B., C.M.G., at the 43rd Training Camp at Barnes and led the march past.

The next large-scale exercise was carried out during the night and early morning of October 10/11, in which 600 all ranks took part. Part of the battalion was attached to the ' enemy ' force and the remainder were defence and counter-attack troops. The London Transport Catering Department provided hot meals during the evening preceding the exercise, after which A Coy. as the ' enemy ' were moved to Manor Park and there snatched a little sleep in street shelters.

At zero hour and under cover of darkness they crossed Wanstead and attacked and captured Ilford Telephone Exchange. Before dawn they had reached Seven Kings, and after hand-to-hand encounters captured the station and consolidated their position. E and D Coys. had meantime been busy defending V.P.s in Plaistow and Wanstead. D Coy. were later called upon to counter-attack to retake Seven Kings station. They were moved by transport to Newbury Park and attacked at once. Team work on both sides was typical of the enthusiasm always shown by the Home Guard on these occasions. A Coy. had not been dislodged by the time ' Cease Fire ' was sounded, soon after dawn. Company cooks had by this time prepared breakfasts for tired, slightly bruised, but happy and hungry Home Guards.

F Coy. combined with a local battalion for a large part of their training. They joined with the Essex Home Guard at Romford in October 1942 for a route march and ceremonial parade before the Lord Lieutenant of the county.

At the invitation of the Mayor of Hackney, Councillor H. Cullington, A Coy. took part in the 'Wings for Victory' parade on March 6, 1943. Under the command of Major S. W. Edis they marched through crowded streets and were later complimented by the Mayor on their smart turn-out. During these winter months Loxford Hall changed considerably. In addition to the general conversion of the house into battalion headquarters and a centre for lectures, much activity took place in the grounds. By May arrangements had been completed to accommodate a maximum of 100 under canvas each week-end. The construction of this training camp was a credit to the pioneer platoon. In addition to the erection of canvas for sleeping and messing, a cook house., ablution shed, etc., were constructed, including the necessary water runs, drains and catch pits. With the exception of the tents, most of these were made from odds and ends of material acquired from various sources. The camp continued throughout the summer and was an outstanding success.

Each company occupied the camp in turn and were responsible for meals and all Q matters, so that in addition to normal field training all companies obtained first-hand Q experience. The training at each camp was provided principally by the incoming company, but special lectures were provided by H.Q. staff. Construction of a miniature range by the Home Guard and a 30-yd. full-bore range by the R.E. was begun but not completed in time for the summer camp.

On April 28, Col. Brook visited D Coy. training quarters at St. Stephen's Hall to present awards during which No. 13 Platoon

(Lieut. Howard) received the Platoon Proficiency Trophy presented by Mr. H. J. Green and Major A. E. Hill ; D Coy. was awarded the Company Proficiency Trophy given by the Battalion Commander.

The following month the King took the salute of the Home Guard in Hyde Park. The 41st contingent of 30 other ranks was led by Lieut. E. Cook, A Coy. and Lieut. W. H. Tott, D Coy. On May 30 London Transport held its third Home Guard anniversary. This time history was really made. Col. Brook arranged for all battalions to assemble at various points in Hyde Park and one by one they converged on the famous cockpit overlooking the Serpentine. Over 3,000 troops on parade were inspected by Lieut. General Sir Arthur Smith, G.O.C. London District, accompanied by Lord Ashfield and Col. Brook. The parade then marched past by platoons in line to the music of the massed bands of the London Transport Home Guard.

North-east London sub-district held a platoon proficiency competition in which the 41st were represented by No. 14 platoon, Forest Gate. The final stages of this hard-fought competition were held at Rainham and Purfleet on September 26. The 51st Essex Batt. won with the 54th Essex Batt. second, and the 41st third. The turn-out of the 41st team earned them top marks in the inspection stage of this competition.

Unfortunately, Lieut. W. H. Tott was taken ill and could not command his platoon, his place being taken at short notice by his 2 i/c, Lieut. F. Donovan. Lieut. Tott died on November 20, and the 41st lost a zealous officer and No. 14 Platoon a popular and hard-working leader.

The Tilston Shield, competed for annually as an individual miniature rifle contest, was won on September 19, 1943, by No. 7946, Cpl. Turner, No. 6 Platoon, B Coy., the runner-up being Pte. Webb of the same platoon. Early in 1944 the Signals Section took part in a competition held by K Sector.

The team of D.R.s entered by the 41st were placed second, Cpl. Butcher gaining the highest individual score in the contest.

In the L.P.T.B. Group Medical contest on February 27, the battalion team reached second place.

The 1944 platoon competition finals held on March 26 resulted in a win for No. 14 Platoon, D Coy., Lieut. H. J. Price, M.M. The final stage of this competition consisted of a five-mile tactical march followed by a fire-and-movement practice on full-bore range.

Fine weather favoured the first drum-head service held at Battalion H.Q. and conducted by the padre, Rev. C. Tatham, on April 30. After the service Col. Brook presented Major Hill with the Company Proficiency Cup which D Coy. had won for the second time. Lieut. Price, No. 14 Platoon, D Coy., received both Platoon Proficiency Cup and Platoon Competition Cup. Led by their pipe band, the battalion later went on a route march, during which Col. Brook took the salute.

The next Home Guard Anniversary was marked by the King taking the salute as they marched through Hyde Park. Lieut. E. Cook, A Coy., led the 41st Batt. with Lieut. L. H. W. Nicholds, also of A Coy.

The L.P.T.B. Group Anniversary Parade was again held in the cockpit at Hyde Park. Sir Charles Lloyd, K.C.B., D.S.O., M.C., now G.O.C. London District, was received by a general salute from 3,000 troops. The service held after the inspection was conducted by the padre of the 44th Batt., the Rev. A. Toller, assisted by the Rev. C. Tatham, O.C.F., padre of the 41st Batt. The 41st Pipe Band paraded with the battalion and provided the music to which the 41st marched past. The G.O.C. was accompanied by Col. Brook, and Mr. John Cliff, representing Lord Ashfield.

Many calls were made on the Home Guard to assist indirectly with the invasion of Europe in June 1944. In addition to many guards and pickets, the 41st will always be proud of the part played by their Signals Section.

Situated as they were in one of the principal transit areas of London, the battalion saw much of the movement of the B.L.A. from the railhead to the London docks. Under the command of Lieut. R. Laws, Battalion Signals Officer, some 22 D.R.s worked with their Regular Army colleagues, and for about three months met and conducted convoys of troops from railhead to transit camps and docks. They gave up their rest days and worked really hard, sometimes being away for 36 hours. Very gratifying compliments were paid to the battalion for these services.

Of the many competitions in which individuals and teams took part, one of the best miniature-rifle team entries was that of No. 1 Platoon, A Coy. The S.M.R.C. National Home Guard team championships for the Mackworth Praed Cup 1944 attracted the record entry of 2,468 teams, each of ten men drawn from all parts of England, Scotland and Wales. The 41st reached the last 25 with a score of 976. In the final shoot they obtained 973, which put them into third place, a splendid effort against great opposition. In the north-east sub-district full-bore rifle competition the battalion reached the finals with the 2nd C.O.L. Batt. after beating many battalions from north-east London. The G.O.C. attended the final at Purfleet and saw the 2nd C.O.L. Batt. win. The 41st were unfortunate to lose the services of one of their good shots owing to a firing pin breaking in the middle of the shoot when only a few plates remained.

Considering their position in the east end of London the battalion were fortunate during the V attacks. There were, of course, several members who lost their homes, some more than once, and a large number suffered damage, but the casualty list was remarkably low, none of the battalion premises receiving major damage except those of D Coy., whose training quarters were destroyed, and whose company offices at West Ham were damaged on two successive week-ends. Many companies gave active assistance to the Civil

Defence services during these attacks, A Coy. in particular receiving many calls and at times performing long hours of duty in the Hackney area.

The record of the battalion would not be complete without mention of their sport and social activities. Many dances and socials were given at battalion, company and platoon levels. The outstanding feature of the sporting side was their cricket team, which played many matches.

The battalion held its stand-down parade at B.H.Q. on November 19, 1944. Following the presentation of Certificates of Merit, Brig. T. Fairfax-Ross, Commanding the N.E.L.S.D., took the salute at the march past in Loxford Lane. Many visitors were later entertained by the mess, including the Brigadier and officers of his staff, Col. Brook and several commanders of other L.P.T.B. battalions.

On December 3, 1944, Lieut. J. S. Bates, D.C.M., M.M., B Coy., and Lieut. G. W. Westcott, C Coy., led the 41st representative unit of 18 other ranks in the central stand-down parade of the whole Home Guard, held in Hyde Park before the King and Queen and both Princesses. The 41st were honoured to be doubly represented by the special inclusion of their pipe band, which led the Scottish contingent.

The following member of the battalion received posthumous commendation in London District Orders :

Pte. W. H. Hewitt.

The following members of the battalion were awarded Certificates of Merit : Major A. E. Hill ; Sgts. A. Parham, S. W. Denny, G. W. Westcott, A Robinson, A. C. Dean, W. H. Eason, C. Johns ; Cpls. G. Attwood, P. Lee, W. Mann ; Ptes. J. C. Old, F. W. Edwards, A. R. Elliot, H. W. Hampshere.

ROLL OF OFFICERS AT 'STAND DOWN'

Name and Rank	*Appointment*
Battalion Headquarters	
Lieut. Col. T. H. Peerless	Officer Commanding
Major T. T. Shephard	Second-in-Command
Major J. A. Moody	Battalion Medical Officer
Capt. C. W. F. Randall	Liaison Officer
Capt. F. J. Buskin	Ammunition Officer
Capt. S. Kaye	Sub-Unit Medical Officer
Capt. W. C. Leaney	Borough Liaison Officer
Lieut. L. W. Richardson	Transport Officer
Lieut. F. E. Johnson	Assistant Quartermaster
Lieut. A. Robinson, M.M.	Gas Officer
Lieut. S. W. Denny	Intelligence Officer
Lieut. R. Laws	Signals Officer
Lieut. R. F. Gessey, M.M.	P.A.D. Officer
Lieut. A. H. Brown	Petrol Disruption Officer
Lieut. W. Jones	Asst. Adjutant and Press Officer
Lieut. W. T. Nutt	Bombing Officer
Lieut. A. E. Whichello	Pioneer Officer
Lieut. C. F. Rawlings	Transport Detachment
Capt. J. D. Canning, H.A.C.	Adjutant
Capt. J. H. Boreham, Royal Fusiliers	Quartermaster
H.Q. Company	
Major P. Beckers	Company Commander
Capt. J. F. Stitfall	Second-in-Command and W.T.O.

Name and Rank	*Appointment*
A Company	
Major S. W. Edis	Company Commander
Capt. A. J. Bourn	Second-in-Command
Lieut. H. Debonnaire	O.C., No. 1 Platoon
Lieut. A. J. Woolmore, D.C.M.	O.C., No. 2 Platoon
Lieut. L. W. Nickolds	O.C., No. 3 Platoon
Lieut. J. R. Barnard	Platoon Officer, No. 3 Platoon
Lieut. E. Cook	O.C., No. 4 Platoon
Lieut. H. J. Manning	Platoon Officer, No. 4 Platoon
2nd Lt. E. S. Cook	Platoon Officer, No. 1 Platoon
2nd Lt. S. W. Howard	Platoon Officer, No. 2 Platoon
B Company	
Major H. G. Cruse	Company Commander
Capt. A Roberts	Second-in-Command
Lieut. J. S. Bates, D.C.M., M.M.	O.C., No. 5 Platoon
Lieut. W. H. Cresswell, M.M.	Platoon Officer, No. 5 Platoon
Lieut. C. H. Mead	O.C., No. 6 Platoon
Lieut. E. W. Payne, M.M.	O.C., No. 7 Platoon
Lieut. W. J. Davis	O.C., No. 8 Platoon
2nd Lt. F. C. Wilson	Platoon Officer No. 7 Platoon
2nd Lt. S. S. Hammond	Platoon Officer No. 8 Platoon
C Company	
Major H. T. Scarborough	Company Commander
Capt. L. T. Howard	Second-in-Command
Lieut. A. T. Moore, D.C.M.	O.C., No. 9 Platoon
Lieut. L. L. Jennings	O.C., No. 10 Platoon
Lieut. G. W. Westcott	O.C., No. 11 Platoon
Lieut. A. E. Silwood	O.C., No. 12 Platoon
Lieut. F. T. Clarke, M.M.	O.C., No. 13 Platoon
2nd Lt. H. E. Chinner	Platoon Officer, No. 9 Platoon
2nd Lt. S. G. Mears	Platoon Officer, No. 10 Platoon
2nd Lt. A. J. Ede, M.M.	Platoon Officer, No. 11 Platoon
2nd Lt. W. H. Bennett	Platoon Officer, No. 13 Platoon

Name and Rank	*Appointment*
D Company	
Major A. E. Hill	Company Commander
Lieut. H. J. Price, M.M.	O.C., No. 14 Platoon
Lieut. F. A. Donovan	Platoon Officer, No. 14 Platoon
Lieut. W. L. Good, M.M.	O.C., No. 15 Platoon
Lieut. A. A. Herbert, M.M.	Platoon Officer, No. 15 Platoon
Lieut. H. F. Woollett	O.C., No. 16 Platoon
Lieut G. Newman, D.C.M.	Platoon Officer, No. 16 Platoon
E Company	
Major J. Cross, M.M.	Company Commander
Capt. W. T. J. King	Second-in-Command
Lieut. W. E. Packham	O.C., No. 17 Platoon
Lieut. C. R. Walker	Platoon Officer, No. 17 Platoon
Lieut. H. A. Mizon	O.C., No. 18 Platoon
Lieut. J. W. May, M.M.	Platoon Officer, No. 18 Platoon
Lieut. W. H. Dodd	O.C., No. 19 Platoon
2nd Lt. C. S. Collins	Platoon Officer, No. 19 Platoon
F Company	
Major C. Chinnery	Company Commander
Lieut. F. Allen	O.C., No. 20 Platoon
Lieut. P. W. Reynolds	O.C., No. 21 Platoon
Lieut. S. R. Simmonds	O.C., No. 22 Platoon
Lieut. F. W. Perry, D.C.M.	O.C., No. 23 Platoon
2nd Lt. C. F. Shurety	Platoon Officer, No. 20 Platoon
2nd Lt. G. Beetlestone	Platoon Officer, No. 21 Platoon
2nd Lt. R. J. Lawrence	Platoon Officer, No. 22 Platoon
Deceased	
Major J. Brady	O.C., C Coy.
Lieut. W. H. Tott	D Coy.

7 The 42nd Battalion

THE staff of the Department of the Chief Mechanical Engineer (Railways) formed the nucleus of the 2nd Batt., forerunner to the 42nd County of London Batt. Acton Works, in which was situated the Headquarters of the L.P.T.B. Unit, early enrolled some 200 men.

Under the guidance of Mr. E. G. Brunker and Mr. T. A. Prentice, squads of 19 men were formed and were later increased to 25 ; on June 24, 1940, the first guards and patrols were mounted for the protection of the works.

By August it was decided to base the command on six battalions. Mr. S. G. Lane, of Acton drawing office, was appointed No. 2 Batt. Commander, and Mr. H. Scarfe became battalion 2 i/c, while the Quartermaster was Mr. J. H. Steele of the solicitor's department. First Adjutant was Mr. C. Wright.

The early history of this unit shows it responsible for the defence of some of London Transport's most vital properties : 55, Broadway, Acton railway works, power houses, sub-station installations and many railway depots. The first battalion headquarters were at Head Office under the 1941 reorganisation. Six companies were formed under the following commands :

A Company
O.C., E. Major ; 2 i/c, C. Withers.
Acton Works
No. 1 Platoon, J. L. Whitfield
No. 2 Platoon, S. P. Jenkins
No. 3 Platoon, G. R. Atkinson
No. 4 Platoon, R. J. Young
B Company
O.C., R. G. Orsman ; 2 i/c, E. Grange
Neasden Depot
No. 5 Platoon, E. Grange
No. 6 Platoon, G. Whitley

Northfields Depot
No. 7 Platoon, J. F. Drake
Hammersmith Depot
No. 8 Platoon, H. J. O'Mara
C Company
O.C., R. H. Liveing ; 2 i/c, J. A. Tucker
Ealing Common
No. 9 Platoon, E. C. Holland
Wood Lane
No. 10 Platoon, J. A. Tucker
Cockfosters
No. 11 Platoon, J. A. Vallance
D Company
O.C., F. Muncey
Golders Green
No. 13 Platoon, C. P. Barber
2 i/c, Bailey
Morden
No. 14 Platoon
E Company
O.C., V. H. Absalom
Leicester Square (Sub-stations)
No. 18 Platoon, W. C. Rose
Greenwich Power House
No. 19 Platoon, W. S. Wood
Lots Road
No. 20 Platoon, J. Scutt
F Company
O.C., G. G. Fisher ; 2 i/c, F. Rose
55, Broadway
No. 21 Platoon, F. Rose
Stanmore
No. 22 Platoon, H. Ham
Hillingdon
No. 23 Platoon, K. Tucker

A long illness during 1940 compelled Mr. R. H. T. Liveing to pass the command of C Coy. to his 2 i/c, Mr. J. Tucker. Upon his return he himself became 2 i/c and also took charge of the Wood Lane Platoon.

Early histories of most Home Guard Battalions are very similar, yet contain such notable distinctions as that recorded in the first year of the 2nd L.P.T.B. Batt. No. 21 Platoon, F Coy., drawn largely from the staff at 55, Broadway, became closely associated with the 1st London Westminster Batt. Home Guard, both for training and operations.

Early in 1941 the 1st Coy., 1st London Batt. received the honour of being detailed to provide the first contingent of Home Guard to take over the King's guard at Buckingham Palace and St. James's.

The depths of friendship and team spirit in the Home Guard was never more eloquently expressed than by Major H. Cowan's immediate invitation to F Coy. to participate in this historic event. Of the many volunteers available eight were finally selected for special training : L/Cpl. F. J. Frost, L/Cpl. A. H. Marsh, L/Cpl. A. S. Parfit, Cpl. H. C. Ruane, Pte. A. F. Manton, Pte. A. E. Walter, Pte. R. H. Rowles and Pte. A. Sibson.

Although selected for their all-round ability and keenness as Home Guards, their knowledge of ceremonial was limited, added to which much polish was needed to do justice to this important duty. They were released from all normal Home Guard duties and joined the 1st Coy., 1st London in concentrated training at Wellington Barracks.

Here they learned the intricacies of Palace Guard changing, and at the same time absorbed a military bearing which only Guards Brigade instructors could produce in such a short space of time. High tributes on the carriage and discipline of all who took part were paid by those whose intimate knowledge of the details of this ceremonial qualified them to be judges.

B Coy., led by Company Commander R. G. Orsman, contained Neasden Depot, which was destined to play a prominent part in the Board's Home Guard. Attention was first drawn to this unit by the visit of General Symonds not many months after their formation, when a smart guard of honour of 34 other ranks, under the command of the company 2 i/c, E. Granve, paraded for their first real Home Guard ceremonial.

This was followed a few weeks later by one of the first inter-company exercises. C Coy., under Company Commander J. Tucker, attacked Neasden Depot under cover of darkness and taught B Coy. many valuable lessons on the methods of attacking and entering a railway depot and power house at night.

Northfields, Hammersmith and Neasden Depots sent contingents regularly to Bisley and also practised consistently on the miniature range at Baker Street. The first inter-platoon miniature rifle contest held by this battalion at Baker Street on May 15, 1941, resulted in F Coy. obtaining first and second places with Neasden Works third.

The early success of C Coy. was due to the support and enthusiasm of Mr. S. Hubbard, of Wood Lane, and to the excellent example set by ' Bob ' Liveing and ' Jimmy ' Tucker. Mr. Holland's personal supervision at all early parades went far to make Ealing Common fit into this well-balanced team.

Cockfosters Depot was more difficult, not through any lack of enthusiasm, but owing to the shift work and the long distances which some of these men lived from their place of work. Even so, they kept pace, and led by Mr. J. A. Vallance carried out guard duties over a large and important area.

Wood Lane drew much attention to themselves by their construction of three strong points and a guard room below ground level. Made from old tunnel segments, these posts not only represented many hours of hard work, but were among the best of their kind and preferable to the familiar roadside block houses.

D Coy., under Company Commander F. Muncey, were fully occupied in training the Board's staff for the defence of railway depots at Golders Green and Morden and from June 1940 onwards guards and patrols were provided nightly.

E Coy., comprising the power station at Greenwich and Lots Road, together with many sub-stations, carried very important re-

sponsibilities which were put to severe tests in exercises. Greenwich power house, because of its importance and geographical position, received the full light of higher command attention from its earliest days and the staff who comprised No. 19 platoon were very much alive to their position. The praise given them by Company Commander V. H. Absalom during their L.D.V. training was more than justified by later events.

In addition to mounting the normal guards nightly, they were called upon from August 1941 onwards to post sentries on the pier as mine watchers. Many were the scares of parachute mines descending into the wide river at this point; so much so that the first sentry who actually saw a mine coming down before him had difficulty in believing his eyes.

After many local tests it was decided to settle once and for all the question of the vulnerability of Greenwich from attack.

On a week-end in October 1941, Greenwich were ordered to prepare for attack. 4.0 p.m. on Saturday the platoon of two officers and 65 other ranks reported at full strength, and were later increased by one officer and 20 other ranks from No. 18 platoon (sub-stations).

This force was kept on the *qui vive* all night without action. The first sight of the 'enemy' was not until 7.4 a.m. on the Sunday. By 12.22 p.m., over 20 hours after reporting for duty, the 'enemy', now known to be drawn from units of two regular infantry battalions, decided to attack their prize target.

Automatic fire from the power house roof,

concentrated on selected approaches, were faithfully recorded by the umpires, and resulted in the first attack withdrawing with 80 per cent. casualties. Almost the entire bombing strength of the defence was located on the roof, the bombs consisting of small bags of whitening.

Gate after gate was attacked without effect, whilst a stronger attack in which an attempt was made to storm the south-west wall gave the same result, except that the Home Guard took two officers and eight other ranks prisoners.

This was at once followed by a much stronger assault on the west wall, which left the attackers looking like millers, and gave the Home Guard another batch of prisoners, whose numbers threatened to become an embarrassment. The regulars now brought Bren carriers against the entrances and never did the Home Guard bombers enjoy themselves more. The white marks on men and vehicles gave eloquent testimony of the bombers' aim. The exercise finished with Greenwich still holding out and the Home Guard ready to ' mix it ' and inquiring when the next test would be.

One realises the full extent of Home Guard enthusiasm when one considers that many

of the participants of this action were continually at work and Home Guard duty for 36 hours without much, if any, sleep.

The activities of the Head Office Home Guard, F Coy., under Mr. G. G. Fisher and Mr. F. Rose, played a prominent part throughout the history of the Unit. The decentralised office staffs at Hillingdon and Stanmore formed platoons based upon these outlying offices under the command of Mr. K. Tucker (since deceased). Despite travelling caused by their decentralisation, they paraded regularly and adapted themselves to a type of warfare far removed from the street fighting with which their Broadway colleagues were grappling.

The re-organisation of the Unit necessitated complete dismemberment of the old battalion. Only Morden Depot remained, the rest being transferred, according to geographical situation, to five other L.P.T.B. battalions.

The new 42nd from November 1, 1941, was based on south-west London, with H.Q. in a requisitioned house at East Sheen. The units transferred in came from every other L.P.T.B. battalion except the 46th. The new commands and organisation were as follows :

	Name and Rank	Appointment
A Company		
	Major V. H. Absalom	Company Commander
	Capt. A. Perrior, C.M.	2nd-in-Command
No. 1 Platoon.	Lieut. A. J. Jennings	Mortlake Garage
No. 2 Platoon.	Lieut. J. C. Castell	Chelverton Road
No. 3 Platoon.	Lieut. A. E. F. Frith	Putney Bridge
No. 4 Platoon.	Lieut. J. S. Watkins	Wandsworth Depot
No. 5 Platoon.	Lieut. A. F. Grinyer	Battersea Garage
B Company		
	Major A. G. Drury	Company Commander
	Capt. W. E. Johnson	2nd-in-Command
No. 6 Platoon.	Lieut. L. Harris	Norwood Garage
No. 7 Platoon.	Lieut. A. E. Grant	Norwood Depot
No. 8 Platoon	Lieut. R. D. Mathias	Streatham Garage
No. 9 Platoon.	Lieut. W. S. Essex	Streatham Depot
C Company		
	Lieut. F. Kearn	Company Commander (afterwards Major)
	Capt. C. W. L. Griffiths	2nd-in-Command
No. 10 Platoon.	Lieut. J. R. Bridger	Croydon Garage
No. 11 Platoon.	Lieut. T. Green	Thornton Heath Depot
No. 12 Platoon.	Lieut. R. C. Holt	Sutton Depot
No. 13 Platoon.	Lieut. A. J. L. Gray	Sutton Garage
D Company		
	Major E. McCracken	Company Commander
	Capt. J. G. Harris	2nd-in-Command
No. 14 Platoon.	Lieut. F. L. Senior	Merton Garage
No. 15 Platoon.	Lieut. R. C. Lamb	Morden Depot
No. 16 Platoon.	Lieut. H. Earl	Morden Station
No. 17 Platoon.	Lieut. E. E. Moss	Kingston Garage
E Company		
	Capt. T. H. Elliott	Company Commander (afterwards Major)
	Lieut. C. Rayner	2nd-in-Command (afterwards Captain)
No. 18 Platoon.	Lieut. A. W. Adams	Chelsham Garage
No. 19 Platoon.	Lieut. H. C. Brimicombe	Godstone Garage
No. 20 Platoon.	Lieut. G. G. Bonner	Reigate Garage
No. 21 Platoon.	Lieut. W. G. B. Edwards	East Grinstead

Capt. C. Wright resigned in the winter of 1941, his position being filled for a short time by Capt. W. Clift and later by the appointment of Capt. A. J. Jennings. Major H. Scarfe relinquished his post on March 25, 1942, and Major Drury became battalion 2 i/c, the command of B Coy. being filled by the promotion of Capt. Johnson with Lieut. A. E. Grant promoted to Captain and Company 2 i/c.

The battalion operational role, at first similar to all others, was later completely altered by the introduction of mobile columns. During the winter of 1941-42 Major Drury placed a scheme before Col. A. Keevil, commanding Z zone, which had for its main purpose the rapid conveyance of small bodies of L.P.T.B. Home Guards to any part of the zone in a counter-attack role. Subsequent interest and guidance given by this enthusiastic Zone Commander built the foundation of the mobile columns which were later to form the main role of the battalion.

Training started at first in B and C Coys., the first demonstration given by C Coy. at Croydon Garage confirming the value of this training and the thought which had been given to the smallest detail. Every man had his own seat on each bus according to his position in the battle platoon and each platoon was completely self-contained. A strict rotation of boarding and ' debussing ' ensured maximum speed in going into action.

Training was later extended to four companies, and as each platoon became efficient columns were formed in more areas ; thus the battalion operational role changed steadily to one of providing small, fast mobile platoons.

In all 22 of these units were raised for service in V, W and Z zones (later sectors), 18 being used directly by the sectors and four held at Morden as sub-district reserve.

The first full-scale exercise was on March 29, 1942. Originally planned for one company, it was finally enlarged to embrace the battalion and became known as the ' Battle of Walton Hill,' in which mobile columns had every opportunity of showing their paces.

Major F. Kearn, C Coy., provided mobile units as demonstration teams who were in operation every month during 1942, 1943 and 1944 in many sectors. They attended the Z sector summer training camp at Nonsuch Park and formed part of the week-end training. Demonstrations to various battalions were also given by teams in B Coy. under Major W. E. Johnson.

In June 1942 the battalion attended the Group anniversary parade held on the Barnes Training Camp ground. After the march past the 42nd Batt. staged a display with a mobile platoon.

Following the re-organisation of 1941 the position of R.S.M. was not filled at once, but early in 1942 R.S.M. J. Lavery was confirmed in his appointment.

Exercise Viper, held over a period of 24 hours in Z sector on August 29/30, called for the full use of B and C Coys., both of which saw fighting against regular troops at Northwood and Thornton Heath.

At the officers' conference held at the Curzon Cinema, W., by the G.O.C. London District, Lieut. Gen. Sir Arthur Smith praised B Coy. and referred particularly to the effective road block formed at a critical moment by the use of two London Transport buses.

September and October of this year saw two important training displays. C Coy., under Major Kearn, staged a counter-attack on an ' enemy '-held road block and houses before a large parade of the 59th Surrey Batt. Home Guard. A Coy., under Major V. H. Absalom, sent units to the south-west sub-district Officers' Training School, where a demonstration was given at the request of Col. J. E. Turner, C.M.G., D.S.O., in order to show unit commanders what they might expect in response to a call for mobile reinforcements. The companies concerned received much praise for their work on both these occasions.

The summer camp at Nonsuch Park formed a prominent part of the 42nd Batt. training. During the summer of 1942 nearly every officer and a high percentage of the N.C.O.s attended these week-end camps. Training was occasionally varied by the co-operation of the R.A.F.

On September 13, when many of the 42nd were in camp, three R.A.F. fighters 'strafed' ' the camp and followed this by a convincing display of accurate low-level bombing.

C Coy. sustained a severe loss when their 2 i/c, Capt. C. W. L. Griffiths was accidentally killed while on civil duty on October 7. A holder of the Territorial Meritorious Medal, Capt. Griffiths was a keen Home Guard and a splendid officer. Lieut. H. J. Giddings,

M.M., was promoted Capt. and Coy. 2 i/c the following March.

In February 1942 Major E. McCracken was granted a regular commission to become Adjutant to the 46th Batt., the 42nd thus lost the services of a very efficient Company Commander. Capt. J. G. Harris received his majority to command D Coy., and Lieut. F. L. Senior was promoted Capt. and Coy. 2 i/c.

By this time 'battle inoculation' or 'assault under fire' had been extended to the Home Guard. This Regular Army toughening-up training required detachments to advance under live fire, all classes of weapons firing on fixed lines, only a few feet above the advancing troops. C Coy. were

the first to participate in this training, and subsequently gave several demonstrations to members of various London and Surrey battalions.

The formation of H.Q. Coy. was sanctioned in February 1943, Capt. J. H. Steele, Quartermaster, being promoted to Major, while Capt. A. H. Passey was transferred in from the 44th Batt. to Coy. 2 i/c.

The Cup presented to the battalion by Mr. J. H. Parker was competed for on an inter-company basis every six months. This contest required teams of eight men to participate in a tactical exercise in which all branches of field training were included.

This was followed by a parade for inspection, foot and arms drill and finally full-bore firing at Bisley. This Cup was won in turn by the following platoons : February 1943—No. 5 Platoon, A Coy. ; September 1943—No. 14 Platoon, D Coy. ; March 1944—No. 2 Platoon, A Coy.

The last contest, in October 1944, was changed to full-bore and revolver shooting at Bisley and was won by E Coy.

The 'Lane Cup' was also competed for every six months. Each company was represented by a team of eight. The first contest in January and February 1943 was held on miniature ranges, but all subsequent contests were full-bore shoots fired at Bisley, the winners being as follows : January 1943— D Coy. ; October 1943—E Coy. ; March 1944—D Coy. ; September 1944—D Coy.

On Sunday, March 21, C Coy. gave one of their demonstrations on mobile column work before Lieut. Gen. Sir Arthur Smith at the South Training Camp, Barnes. The use of an epidiascope enabled details of the position of each man to be clearly portrayed before seeing the team at work. Many visiting officers from other L.P.T.B. Batts. were present.

Lieut. A. V. Wood, Asst. Quartermaster, had covered all Q duties since the promotion of Capt. Steele, and on April 24, 1943, he was granted a regular commission and became Quartermaster with the rank of Captain, a position he retained until after the stand down.

One of the most outstanding features in the history of the 42nd Batt. was the amazing shooting record of D Coy. Their successes in the full-bore competitions have already been mentioned, and the miniature range team led by Capt. (later Major) F. Senior included such crack shots as Sgts. Neville, Pets and Spirate and L/Cpls. Brush and Spratley, supported by an unusually large number of more than average shots.

This team fired both as a company and battalion team, but on the latter occasions usually included men from other companies. They went from success to success against both Home Guard teams and representative teams of famous regiments. Some picture of their record may be gained from the following summary of victories on miniature ranges both in and out of London.

Forty matches won against other Home Guard Companies or Battalions from London, Surrey and Sussex included one over the 45th Batt. team, who were at that time winners of the N.R.A. Home Guard Competition.

Six Metropolitan Police teams and the Norbury and Wimbledon Police teams were beaten, as were H.M. Grenadier, Scots and Coldstream Guards and the Royal Marines at Chatham.

The battalion lost their Medical Officer in 1943, when Major J. Sayers was called to the Regular Army on October 16. Capt. I. Hammel, B Coy. M.O., became battalion M.O. with the rank of Major.

In November 1943 the 42nd Batt. promoted a full-bore competition between officers of all L.P.T.B. battalions and Unit Headquarters.

The contest, held at Bisley, was won by the 42nd Batt. with the 60th London Batt. as runners-up. In September 1944, the contest was held again, but on this occasion the 60th London Batt. won on a very cold and wintry day, with the 42nd Batt. runners-up.

The winter training of 1943-44 was based largely on an inter-Platoon Quiz Competition arranged by Major A. Drury. Teams of eight men represented each platoon. Teams drawn against each other assembled at selected training quarters and sat opposite each other. Questions based entirely on Home Guard training were then put in the usual 'quiz' manner, the gong being sounded after 30 secs. Many spectators attended these contests, during which each contestant was asked three questions. Every platoon entered, and it can be estimated how much work was entailed to avoid repetition of questions. In all, Major Drury prepared over 1,000 questions, all based on Home Guard training. The finals, held at Tooting in March 1944 resulted as follows : 1st, No. 15 Platoon—Morden Depot, D Coy.; 2nd, No. 4 Platoon—Wandsworth (Trams), A Coy. ; 3rd, No. 2 Platoon—Chelverton Road (Buses), A Coy.

An important battalion church parade was held at Tooting Parish Church on Sunday, February 23, 1944, conducted by the Rev. R. R. Neill, M.A. The service was attended by the G.O.C. London District, Lieut. Gen. Sir Arthur Smith, who read the lesson and gave an address. After the service the G.O.C. took the salute of the battalion as they marched away, headed by the band of the 44th Batt.

Major J. G. Harris relinquished his command of D Coy. in May 1944, and was succeeded by his 2 i/c, Capt. F. L. Senior, who received his majority.

The appointment of Lieut. A. F. Grinyer to Capt. and 2 i/c, A Coy. had appeared in orders during the previous month, whilst the vacancy now created by the promotion of Capt. Senior was filled in the following month, when Lieut. W. D. Gowler became Capt. and 2 i/c, D Coy.

A battalion battle platoon entered the inter-battalion contest for the 'Brook Cup' and gained second place. Led by Lieut. T. McElligott of C Coy., the team paraded in miserable weather at Hedgerley Park on April 2, 1944, and went through ceremonial inspection and tactical field work with enthusiasm. Covered in mud, they reached the full-bore 200 yd. range more than an hour after leaving the parade ground and were then immediately engaged with snap targets appearing at any point along the butts.

The Director-General of the Home Guard, Major-Gen. Lord Bridgeman, C.B., D.S.O., M.C., attended and presented the Cup before a large gathering of officers of both the Regular Army and Home Guard.

The gallantry of several members of the battalion during the V attacks on London has already been mentioned in earlier chapters, but the history of the battalion would be incomplete without mentioning one very brave life-saving act.

Sgt. Barrell of A Coy. received the Royal Humane Society's certificate for saving the life of a child. He was having tea before going on Home Guard duty when he heard that a child had fallen into a static water tank nearby. Still in uniform, Sgt. Barrell reached the tank, dived in and saved the child. His certificate was presented by the Mayor of Battersea.

L/Cpl. Drew received a similar certificate from Mr. Claude Mullins at Wandsworth Police Court for saving a man of 40 who had fallen into an emergency water tank. This rescue was made more difficult by the struggles of the man and for some moments it was a dangerous situation for the L/Cpl. Fortunately his powerful build enabled him to prevail. His award also took into consideration that he had previously saved the life of a small boy in yet another static water tank.

Much of the battalion area was in 'Doodle Bug Alley', and all companies assisted the hard-pressed Civil Defence forces. Not least of these efforts were those of No. 4 Platoon, A Coy., who worked repeatedly near their headquarters under their leader, Lieut. L. Shaw, supported by Sgt. Chippett and L/Cpl. Drew.

C Coy. received many calls for assistance, to one of which every man on parade was sent in response to a call from Lieut. Col. Waller of Z sector.

Major W. E. Johnson was injured when B Coy. Headquarters were completely wrecked on July 27, 1944.

The stand down of the Home Guard curtailed further organised assistance, but many individuals continued to give assistance wherever possible.

The 42nd mustered as a battalion for the last time on Sunday, November 5, 1944, at Tooting Bec Common and marched to the Parish Church. The service was conducted by the Rev. R. R. O'Neill, and the lesson read by the Batt. 2 i/c, Major A. G. Drury. Lieut. Col. S. G. Lane took the salute of his battalion as they marched away to dismiss.

In the final stand-down parade the 42nd contingent was led by Major W. E. Johnson, O.C., B Coy. and Lieut. W. A. Buckle, No. 7 Platoon, B Coy.

Certificates of Merit awarded to members of the battalion were received by the following : L/Cpl. J. H. Dunt, Pte. H. L. Davidson, Pte. P. H. Vale, Cpl. C. East, Pte. H. W. A. Duckett, Sgt. S. P. Jones, Cpl. W. Golding, Pte. J. G. Wrigley, Capt. A. J. Jennings, Pte. F. Keating, Pte. G. S. Wilkin, Sgt. A. Mansell, Sgt. C. Courtness and Sgt. F. Thurogood.

ROLL OF OFFICERS AT 'STAND DOWN'

Name and Rank	*Appointment*
Battalion Headquarters	
Lieut. Col. S. G. Lane	Officer Commanding
Major A. G. Drury	Second-in-Command
Major I. Hammel	Batt. Medical Officer
Capt. G. C. Vine	Liaison Officer
Capt. S. A. Webb	Ammunition Officer
Capt. L. J. Lavery	Weapon Training Officer
Lieut. E. Holt	Transport Officer
Lieut. A. J. L. Gray	Assistant Quartermaster
Lieut. J. H. Browne	Camouflage Officer
Lieut. G. C. D. Deadman	Gas Officer
Lieut. F. R. Day	Intelligence Officer
Lieut. E. Payne	Signals Officer
Lieut. C. G. Olney	P.A.D. Officer
Lieut. S. J. Warner	Petrol Dis. Officer and Press Officer
Lieut. F. Lee	Bombing Officer
Lieut. W. E. Smith	Pioneer Officer
Lieut. W. J. J. Roberts	P.T. Officer
Lieut. L. H. Scott	Messing Officer
Capt. A. J. Jennings, Gen.List	Adjutant
Capt. A. V. Wood, Gen. List	Quartermaster

LIEUTENANT-COLONEL S. G. LANE AND SENIOR OFFICERS

Name and Rank   *Appointment*

H.Q. Company
Major J. H. Steele   Company Commander
Capt. A. H. Passey   Second-in-Command

A Company
Major C. M. Perrior   Company Commander
Capt. A. F. Grinyer   Second-in-Command
Lieut. E. J. Winsbarrow   O.C., No. 1 Platoon
Lieut. W. Stalham   O.C., No. 2 Platoon
Lieut. A. E. F. Frith   O.C., No. 3 Platoon
Lieut. L. H. Shaw   O.C., No. 4 Platoon
Lieut. F. W. Pluck   O.C., No. 5 Platoon
2nd Lt. F. G. Crandley   Platoon Officer, No. 1 Platoon
2nd Lt. E. Pike   Platoon Officer, No. 2 Platoon
2nd Lt. C. Willis   Platoon Officer, No. 3 Platoon
2nd Lt. W. G. Aldridge   Platoon Officer, No. 4 Platoon
2nd Lt. A. P. C. Willis   Platoon Officer, No. 5 Platoon

B Company
Major W. E. Johnson   Company Commander
Capt. A. E. Grant   Second-in-Command
Lieut. A. J. Slade   O.C., No. 6 Platoon
Lieut. W. A. Buckle   O.C., No. 7 Platoon
Lieut. W. H. Adams   Platoon Officer, No. 7 Platoon
Lieut. R. D. Mathias   O.C., No. 8 Platoon
Lieut. W. H. Day   Platoon Officer, No. 8 Platoon
Lieut. G. A. Windaybank   O.C., No. 9 Platoon
Lieut. W. S. Essex   Platoon Officer, No. 9 Platoon
2nd Lt. T. D. Adams   Platoon Officer, No. 6 Platoon
2nd Lt. W. G. C. Davis   Platoon Officer, No. 6 Platoon
2nd Lt. H. C. Rockliffe   Platoon Officer, No. 9 Platoon

C Company
Major F. Kearn   Company Commander
Capt. H. J. Giddings   Second-in-Command
Lieut. J. R. Bridger   O.C., No. 10 Platoon
Lieut. T. E. McElligott   O.C., No. 11 Platoon
Lieut. C. R. Brazier   O.C., No. 12 Platoon
Lieut. J. Maher   O.C., No. 13 Platoon
2nd Lt. S. G. Smith   Platoon Officer, No. 10 Platoon
2nd Lt. E. C. Ravenswood   Platoon Officer, No. 10 Platoon
2nd Lt. R. L. Hayes   Platoon Officer, No. 11 Platoon
2nd Lt. C. A. Pearson   Platoon Officer, No. 11 Platoon
2nd Lt. J. D. Nimmo   Platoon Officer, No. 12 Platoon
2nd Lt. B. R. Lomer   Platoon Officer, No. 13 Platoon

Name and Rank	Appointment
D Company	
Major F. L. Senior	Company Commander
Capt. W. D. Gouler	Second-in-Command
Lieut. T. A. Goard	O.C., No. 14 Platoon
Lieut. R. C. Lamb	O.C., No. 15 Platoon
Lieut. H. C. Price	O.C., No. 16 Platoon
Lieut. E. E. Moss	O.C., No. 17 Platoon
Lieut. A. G. Goddard	Platoon Officer, No. 17 Platoon
2nd Lt. A. E. Jolliffe	Platoon Officer, No. 14 Platoon
2nd Lt. F. H. W. Barnett	Platoon Officer, No. 14 Platoon
2nd Lt. H. W. Lane	Platoon Officer, No. 16 Platoon
2nd Lt. J. Gibb	Platoon Officer, No. 15 Platoon
E Company	
Major T. H. Elliott	Company Commander
Capt. C. Rayner	Second-in-Command
Lieut. W. E. Dawes	O.C., No. 19 Platoon
Lieut. R. I. Proctor	O.C., No. 20 Platoon
2nd Lt. A. G. Whittle	Platoon Officer, No. 18 Platoon
2nd Lt. F. C. Bryant	Platoon Officer, No. 20 Platoon
2nd Lt. J. E. Brooks	Platoon Officer, No. 21 Platoon

8 The 43rd Battalion

BY FAR the largest unit in the Board's L.D.V. was that formed from the operating and engineering staffs of the buses and coaches north of the Thames. It was known at first as the 3rd Batt., and early administration was in the hands of Mr. J. H. Williams, Equipment Engineer, who, as Assistant Group Organiser, handled the enrolment of over 5,000 men in this battalion. In addition to its great numbers the unit presented a serious problem in control, the area covered being about 1,000 square miles—roughly half the total area of the Board's vast organisation. Each garage was a self-contained platoon and there were 49 of them. Strengths varied from 30 in the smaller premises to platoons of 300 in the large central area garages. The appointment of Mr. H. K. Cleary as Battalion Commander marked the beginning of real military organisation. This enthusiastic Australian established his first headquarters in a small office at Hammersmith bus garage. From this small beginning great progress was made. It was impossible to handle adequately a large battalion from such a small office, and headquarters were later moved to Chiswick old tram depot. Starting with a desk in a warden's office, the battalion H.Q. was constantly extended until it proved to be one of the most satisfactory headquarters in the Unit.

Mr. E. D. Peaty, assistant to Mr. J. H. Williams, was largely responsible for the 3rd and 4th Batt. records. Following the formation of companies, Mr. Peaty was appointed battalion 2 i/c. Three companies were formed and coincided with the Board's divisional boundaries. A Coy.—Mr. J. B. Woodward, covered C Division central buses.

B Coy.—Mr. J. J. Honnor, B Division central buses. C Coy.—Mr. T. T. Shephard, D Division (North) country buses and coaches. The early organisation was:

A Company—Dollis Hill

No. 1 Plat.	Dollis Hill	E. J. O'Neill
No. 2 Plat.	Holloway	A. Brown
No. 4 Plat.	Chalk Farm	R. Dudley
No. 6 Plat.	Cricklewood	R. Eyre
No. 8 Plat.	Hammersmith	T. Storey
No. 9 Plat.	Hanwell	
No. 10 Plat.	Mortlake	C. W. Perrior
No. 11 Plat.	Willesden	H. J. Mackay
No. 12 Plat.	Alperton	C. Cates
No. 13 Plat.	Potters Bar	R. J. Kenyon
No. 14 Plat.	Hounslow	A. Kettle
No. 15 Plat.	Turnham Grn.	J. Cracknell
No. 16 Plat.	Hendon	E. G. Abbott
No. 17 Plat.	Middle Row	E. H. Robertson
No. 18 Plat.	Harrow Weald	S. A. Blake
No. 19 Plat.	Victoria	B. C. Smith
No. 20 Plat.	Edgware	W. Brine
No. 21 Plat.	Kingston	E. E. Moss
No. 22 Plat.	Shepherds Bush	A. Hatt
No. 23 Plat.	Uxbridge	S. H. Piggott
No. 24 Plat.	Twickenham	. Macefield

Adjutant—E. J. O'Neill

B Company—Kingsland Road

No. 1 Plat.	Dalston	E. White
No. 2 Plat.	Hackney	T. Downey
No. 3 Plat.	Athol Street	J. Davis
No. 4 Plat.	Clay Hall	A. Bourn
No. 5 Plat.	Kingsland Rd.	S. Edis
No. 6 Plat.	Loughton	J. Stevens
No. 7 Plat.	Leyton	A. W. Turner
No. 8 Plat.	Tottenham	A. F. Franks
No. 9 Plat.	West Green	W. Carroll
No. 10 Plat.	Enfield	G. S. Hooles
No. 11 Plat.	Palmers Green	J. Dennis
No. 12 Plat.	Muswell Hill	H. Ashton
No. 13 Plat.	Seven Kings	W. T. King
No. 14 Plat.	Forest Gate	F. Donovan
No. 15 Plat.	Upton Park	P. Beckers
No. 16 Plat.	Barking	P. D. Smith
No. 17 Plat.	Hornchurch	J. Smith

A. and Q.—R. H. Furner

C Company—Lambeth
Platoon Commander—H. A. Walker

No. 1 Plat. Watford High St. L.A. Simmonds
No. 2 Plat. Watford
     (Leavesden Rd.) A. E. Johnson
No. 3 Plat. Hemel
     Hempstead A. Chapman
No. 4 Plat. Tring   A. Saunders
     Plat. Com.   W. Randall
No. 5 Plat. Amersham   J. Hazell
No. 6 Plat. High Wycombe A. Duff
     Plat. Com.   H. G. Knowles
No. 7 Plat. St. Albans   C. Wheeler
No. 8 Plat. Hertford   S.A. Thompson
No. 9 Plat. Hatfield   E. E. Boseley
No. 10 Plat. Luton   H. Trussell
     Plat. Com.   J. Withers
No. 11 Plat. Romford   H. Course
No. 12 Plat. Grays   W. G. Turner
No. 13 Plat. Epping   F. W. Perry
     A. and Q.—W. Webb

In addition, Mr. R. Hill took over duties of Weapon Training Officer.

Following the appeal for volunteers for general service, some 3,000 names were received. Whilst it might have been ultimately necessary to call on these men, it was not the intention of the Home Guard Directorate or London Transport to allow such a high proportion to be withdrawn from London Transport's defences. Every platoon, therefore, selected men by age and ability for this service. Gradually these forces were fitted into a general defence plan of the northern half of London. The largest became known as the L.P.T.B. Composite Batt. It first appeared in January 1941 and contained six platoons of the 3rd Batt. in addition to six from other L.P.T.B. battalions. Their task was to occupy part of the first line of the extreme western defence of London. This was followed by the formation of the London Transport Coy. Centred on Hammersmith bus garage, this company was formed from four platoons of the 3rd Batt. and three from other battalions. Attached to F zone, Chiswick Coy., they were responsible for the defence of two Thames bridges in the Chiswick area.

In common with the remainder of the Home Guard, the 3rd Batt. received their County name in March 1941 and became the 43rd County of London (L.P.T.B.) Batt. The 43rd made their first ceremonial appearance in Chiswick, when, on May 17, 1941, they participated in a large parade of all services for 'War Weapons Week'. The guard of honour at the saluting base was also provided by the 43rd, under the command of Lieut. J. Cracknell. A few weeks previously B Coy. of the 43rd had held their first big parade, led by Major J. J. Honnor. They marched past Col. Stuart Mallinson, C.B.E., D.S.O.. M.C., who took the salute outside Kingsland Road B·divisional offices. A particularly efficient guard of honour, led by Platoon Commander Roberts, received the reviewing officer upon his arrival. The parade which followed was held in a thunderstorm. The inspection went on uninterrupted despite the rain and the counter attraction of a nearby barrage balloon being struck by lightning and falling in flames. Soaked through to the skin the men were dismissed in bright sunshine.

On Saturday, May 7, the 43rd were represented at the first anniversary parade at Osterley. This parade was notable for the first appearance of the Unit Band, led by Lieut. Monk. This band had been formed within the 43rd Batt. The following day—Sunday—May 8, there was a parade which proved to be the largest ever held within one battalion. It was certainly the largest company parade in the whole of the L.P.T.B. Unit and most probably in the whole of the Home Guard—just over 700 all ranks. A Coy., who were responsible for this, paraded at the Sports Ground at Cricklewood, kindly lent by the L.M.S. Col. G. S. Hussey, M.C., and Lieut. Col. G. N. Ford, O.B.E., of the L.M.S., attended. Gen. A. Symons, C.M.G., took the salute in company with Col. Brook, and many visiting officers. The band made its second appearance at this parade and played for the march past, which was carried out in platoons-in-line before re-forming and advancing as company-in-line in accordance with strict ceremonial.

The very scattered layout of C Coy. made large parades difficult. The country area covered by this company enabled field exercises to be a regular training feature. Major T. T. Shephard encouraged the closest liaison with the Hertfordshire, Buckinghamshire and Essex Home Guard, who were responsible for C Coy.'s platoons in battle. Of the many joint exercises with these units, none created greater satisfaction and amusement than that in which St. Albans platoon was pitted against the local

Home Guard. The 'enemy' were allowed transport, for which purpose buses were supplied. During the action, St. Albans captured one of these buses. Platoon Commander C. Wheeler at once drove the bus to 'enemy' headquarters, and by considerable cunning contrived to have a platoon of the 'enemy' loaded on his bus without disclosing his identity. The platoon started on their comfortable journey to the 'front' and realised too late their predicament when deposited amongst the St. Albans men, well inside C Coy's area.

In common with the remainder of the battalion, C Coy. mounted guards nightly at all the country garages, each platoon hoping that their area would be the first to see the 'parachutes'. Hertfordshire Platoon, under Platoon Commander Thompson, certainly had this distinction. One night in the early days of the blitz the guard had been posted, a raid was in progress, and several times enemy aircraft passed overhead. There was nothing unusual in that and the guard room remained peaceful until suddenly swept into action by the shouts of the sentry — 'Guard turn out — parachutes descending'. The guard turned out in a flash, fixed bayonets, and led by the guard commander, advanced at the double to where the sentry had plainly seen a parachute descending against the night sky; the next second none of them knew what had happened — they were still alive, but there appeared to have been an earthquake. The parachute had been attached to a mine. Fortunately the guard sustained no casualties.

In the reorganisation of November 1941 the 43rd Batt. almost ceased to exist. Only four of the original 49 garages remained in the new structure. Necessary as it was to reduce the size of this battalion, it was a great disappointment to Lieut. Col. H. K. Cleary to lose such a large part of a unit which he had done so much to create. Amongst the officers lost by this transfer were all the original company commanders. The

O.C., A Coy., had been promoted Lieut. Col. to command the newly formed 60th. Major J. J. Honnor resigned owing to ill-health, and Major T. T. Shephard became 2 i/c of the 41st Batt. The new battalion organisation was : A Coy.—Major G. H. Gillman, Capt. J. W. Ayris (Chiswick Works) ; B Coy. —Major A. V. Bond, Capt. W. Tarling (Ravenscourt Park Station, Hammersmith Met. Station, Wood Lane Depot, Wood Lane Station, Parsons Green Building Dept.) ; C Coy.—Major J. Cracknell, Capt. R. Houlgrave (Chiswick Old Tram Depot, Hammersmith Garage, Shepherds Bush Garage, Hammersmith Depot) ; and D Coy.—Major G. G. Fisher, Capt. F. D. Rose (55, Broadway, Lots Road Power Station, Victoria Garage, Charing Cross Station).

The only change in company command was in A Coy. In April 1942 Major G. H. Gillman relinquished his post and Capt. J. W. Ayris received his majority and commanded A Coy. until the stand down. Early the following year Lieut. E. M. Price was promoted Captain and 2 i/c.

The work of the battalion in general, and its Battalion Commander in particular, now received a due mark of appreciation. In the Birthday Honours for this year, Lieut. Col. H. K. Cleary was awarded the O.B.E.

Capt. D. G. Brown, M.C., who had succeeded Capt. M. K. Foster as Adjutant (unpaid) in January 1942, remained with the battalion until August 1943, but handed over to Lieut. E. J. Davies (Pioneer Corps) on March 26, 1943, when the latter was posted to the battalion as Regular Adjutant.

The first battalion parade of the new 43rd was attended by nearly 500 officers and other ranks and they marched to Christ Church, Turnham Green, on February 22, 1942. Church parades were held regularly throughout the history of the battalion. Their Padre, the Rev. S. Osborne-Goodchild, A.K.C., always officiated ; on this occasion the 43rd Batt. band made its first appearance.

In accordance with War Office instructions · all factory volunteer bomb disposal units were absorbed into the Home Guard during the winter of 1942/43. The L.P.T.B. unit at Chiswick Works accordingly became part of the 43rd Batt. in February 1943. Their leader, Sgt. G. W. Matthews, was commissioned in the following August and led his splendid team on several occasions to assist the 24th Coy. B.D.U., Royal Engineers, in taking out unexploded enemy bombs in the Brentford and Shepherds Bush areas.

The steady increase in the size and efficiency of specialist sub-units made it very necessary to co-ordinate these services under one command. The formation of a H.Q. Coy. was accordingly applied for and authorised. Capt. F. D. Rose, 2 i/c D Coy., was promoted Major on September 28, 1942, and took over the formation of this company. Four new platoons were made : No. 18 Signals, Scouts and Guides ; No. 20 Medical ; and No. 21 Pioneers and Band. The fourth platoon, No. 19, was formed at the suggestion of the Commander, Col. Brook, and recruited its main strength from officers of London Transport and their assistants. Part 2 Batt. Orders for October 25, 1942, giving the formation of new companies, contained amongst the other ranks a list of names which might at first be mistaken for an extract from the list of members in the higher degrees of the Institute of Transport.

Although realising that their important

positions in the control of London's civilian road and rail transport might preclude them from taking an active part in the primary call-out of the Home Guard, the members of this platoon showed the keenest activity in all branches of training. No. 19 Platoon had a high appreciation of military discipline. It would be difficult to find greater examples of the democratic spirit of the Home Guard than those provided by this unit. A parade containing the heads of departments or divisions of a great business organisation sprang to attention at the entry of one of their signal fitters who happened to be an officer. They gave close attention to a lecture by one of their lift attendants—the battalion Gas N.C.O. Had it been necessary for the 43rd Batt. to fight, the excellent marksmanship of No. 19 Platoon would have taken heavy toll of the enemy.

The operational role of the 43rd was very clearly defined. From being the most scattered unit they were now more compact than any other battalion in London Transport. Centred on Chiswick, the battalion, less D Coy. (55, Broadway) and No. 11 Platoon (Shepherds Bush), defended the Chiswick river area and continued their association with the two river bridges. Unlike so many utility units, they were not split up for operations, but continued as one battalion under Lieut. Col. H. K. Cleary. No. 11 Platoon, although attached for action to F Sector Chiswick Coy., remained in close contact with their colleagues by defending the area colloquially known as ' The Bend '. D Coy. (55, Broadway) were from start to finish attached to the 1st London (Westminster) Batt. for operations.

A pleasant contrast to normal duty befell an honoured few of D Coy. when they were selected to participate in the King's Guard at Buckingham Palace. This was the second occasion when the Home Guard had been so honoured. D Coy., originally in the 42nd Batt., were invited to join with the 1st Coy. of the 1st London (Westminster) in

LIEUTENANT-COLONEL H. K. CLEARY, O.B.E., WITH HIS SENIOR
BATTALION OFFICERS

1941 and again in 1943. The hours spent under strict supervision of the Guards Warrant Officers were enthusiastically given up by all those selected. The Home Guard had occasion to be proud of the way these men, with the 1st London Batt., upheld the high standard.

The highlight of the 43rd training was their camp. Opening on April 26, 1942, on the United Services Staff Sports Grounds at Chiswick, this centre formed the king-pin of every branch of training throughout the battalion. The success of this camp was due to the drive and enthusiasm of all ranks within the battalion, not least the Battalion Commander himself. The camp later became known as 'The London Transport South Training Centre', and provided facilities for four L.P.T.B. battalions. Of the many efficiency competitions held at this centre none was more keenly contested than that held on August 30, 1942. No. 13 Platoon, D Coy., under Lieut. H. W. Webb, won by a narrow margin after a very keen struggle, and received the Platoon Aggregate Cup presented by Staff Sgt. W. W. Bryan. On the same day the 43rd staged a most ambitious sports meeting, which proved to be one of the most successful athletic competitions ever held in the London Transport Home Guard.

A Coy. (Chiswick Works), under Major J. W. Ayris, won the Coy. Cup presented by Major G. G. Fisher, D Coy. Their success was largely due to the keenness shown by Chiswick Works in the London Transport peace-time athletic championships. The miniature range built at the camp assisted largely in the initial training of the large numbers of all ranks who visited Bisley regularly. It is not surprising that the standard of shooting in the battalion was particularly high.

In the difficult Lockboisdale Trophy the 43rd ran into 15th place, a very creditable performance considering the magnitude of this competition.

In the Home Guard war course of 1944 two members of the battalion were included in the very select band of marksmen designated the 'Home Guard Hundred'. They were L/Cpl. G. Laws and Lieut. G. R. Aldridge, who scored 133 and 132 respectively out of a possible 140. Thirty-nine officers and other ranks obtained the marksman degree entitling them to wear the appropriate badge. One hundred and sixteen qualified as service shots. These numbers represented a high proportion of those able to participate in the full course.

Through the generosity of Messrs. Symington & Co., Ltd., and the kind offices of the Mayor of Hammersmith, the battalion acquired their own mobile canteen during 1943. Fully equipped to serve large quantities of hot soups, this vehicle proved of welcome assistance at many exercises and tactical marches.

The cup presented by Mr. V. A. M. Robertson was competed for regularly as an inter-platoon miniature-rifle contest. The first winners in April 1943 were No. 19 Platoon, D Coy., who beat No. 16 Platoon, D Coy., by 33 points. In the second contest several months later No. 19 Platoon were winners again, with No. 16 Platoon 30 points behind. The tenacity of No. 16 Platoon was rewarded in June 1944 when they won deservedly against the champions, who were again in the final. Thus did the officers of various departments of London Transport battle for this coveted trophy against even the humblest members of the staff.

Training in the heavier weapons, particularly sub-artillery, reached its zenith when, in company with batteries from F sector, the 43rd sent their Smith guns and Spigot mortars to Chobham Ridges for a full day of field firing. Very few opportunities for full range sub-artillery live firing were available to any London battalion. The 43rd and 60th shared the distinction of being the two L.P.T.B. battalions given allocations for this excellent and very real training.

The compactness of the 43rd enabled them to hold battalion parades more easily than their colleagues, and so their records contained more than the average number of battalion parades and marches. They were always fully represented at the group parades, the second of which was held on their own training ground. Their longest marches were usually from battalion headquarters to the training ground and back, a distance of some six miles. The first of these was held

on October 4, 1942, when many favourable comments were made on the bearing of the men at the end of the march, despite their considerable variations in age.

On April 18, 1943, the battalion again marched from battalion headquarters to their camp and back. A feature of these marches was the training demonstration staged at the camp during the halt, the subjects varying from gas instruction to unarmed combat.

The battalion M.O., Major G. Morgan Evans, was promoted Lieut. Col. and Group Medical Advisor on August 17, 1943. Capt. J. L. Thomas, sub-unit Medical Officer thus became Major and battalion Medical Officer.

On Saturday, August 21, 1943, Lieut. W. C. Rose, M.M., passed away in a military hospital after being taken ill while attending a training school. Aged 47, Lieut. Rose was a member of the Chief Electrical Engineer's Department at Baker Street. He had received the M.M. whilst serving with the Buffs in the first world war. His conscientious service with the Home Guard and his constant attendance at every possible lecture and training course made him a most valuable officer. By his untimely death No. 16 Platoon (Sub-stations) lost a keen leader and a good friend.

The Home Guard rarely came in contact with our American allies during their training, but the 43rd took every opportunity to entertain any members of the U.S.A. forces. One of these occasions was a full-bore rifle match between a U.S.A. Army team and a Home Guard team from Nos. 9 and 11 platoons, led by Lieut. W. G. Hornsey. Held at Wormwood Scrubbs, this contest produced a high standard of shooting, the 43rd scoring 939 and the U.S.A. team 846. The visitors were later entertained at Shepherds Bush Platoon H.Q.

The resumption of intensive enemy aerial activities in February 1944 found the Home Guard ready. Heavy bombing in the vicinity of B Coy. H.Q. wrecked many houses and also smashed the windows and started a fire at B Coy. The guard dealt with the fire

and were then instrumental in recovering two people from the debris on the wrecked third floor of an adjoining house. This rescue entailed appreciable personal risk and required considerable agility. The light of day later showed just how hazardous their task had been. This team was led by Pte. L. Davies, who acted with commendable initiative and promptitude.

On April 2, 1944, the 43rd participated in the Brook Cup Inter-Battalion contest held at Hedgerley Park. Their battle platoon was led by Lieut. L. J. Manwaring, of No. 16 platoon. This strenuous and comprehensive contest called for a very high standard of all-round efficiency and fitness. The 43rd were placed third after running the 42nd Batt. very close for second place. The contest was won by the 60th Batt. The standard reached by this platoon during its intensive training was largely due to the enthusiastic leadership of Lieut. Manwaring. The fine physique and hard work of this young officer had brought him from the ranks to unarmed combat officer and thence to O.C., No. 16 Platoon. He had for five years held the London Transport high jump championship. His death seven months later was a severe blow to the battalion, and

for the second time No. 16 Platoon lost their leader. Lieut. Manwaring was greatly missed.

On June 2, 1944, the battalion, headed by their band, marched into the cockpit at Hyde Park to participate in what proved to be the last Group anniversary parade. As Lieut. Col. H. K. Cleary, O.B.E., led his battalion past the saluting base he had every reason to be proud of the 400 officers and men behind him. With bayonets fixed, the battalion were a striking testimony to the enormous amount of time and work put in by all ranks.

Anticipating the stand down of the Home Guard and wishing to thank his battalion for their work, Lieut. Col. Cleary called officers and men together on Sunday, October 15, 1944. The parade of over 400 all ranks was inspected by Brig. F. A. F. Capland Griffiths, D.S.O., M.C., commanding south-west London sub-district, in company with Col. Brook. The brigadier's words of appreciation of the work done by the Home Guard were very clearly heard by all ranks owing to the efforts of 2nd Lt. C. V. Taylor and Sgt. Earl, who obtained microphones and loudspeaker units and wired up the parade ground. The battalion, headed by its band, then marched to Hammersmith Town Hall,

BRIGADIER F. A. F. COPLAND-GRIFFITHS, D.S.O., M.C., INSPECTING
'A' COMPANY 43RD BATTALION

where they were received by the Mayor, Alderman Woods, and the Mayor-elect, Councillor Broder. In his address, Lieut. Col. Cleary recorded his personal thanks and appreciation for the fine work accomplished by all ranks under his command during the four years, and stressed the excellent spirit of comradeship built up during this time. Col. Brook presented Certificates of Merit before speaking to the battalion and also handed silver spoons to the 39 officers and other ranks who had qualified as marksmen. In his remarks the unit commander endorsed the battalion commander's words and laid stress on the number of men it had been his pleasure to meet through the Home Guard— a pleasure he would not have known under peace-time conditions even though they were all members of the same vast organisation.

The Mayor of Hammersmith paid high tribute to the men of the battalion when speaking with deep feeling of their assistance to the Civil Defence during the blitz and flying-bomb attacks. The battalion later re-formed and marched through the district; the salute was taken by their C.O.

A further honour came to the battalion when it was represented by personnel of D Coy. in the guard of the Unknown Warrior's Tomb. D Coy. provided part of this unit on four successive years. The quiet efficiency of the 'civilian soldiers' in this most impressive ceremonial role was commented on by men and women of all countries who were privileged to see it. In 1943 eleven of the 20 necessary were provided by the 43rd—a technical assistant, eight clerks and two advertisement hands. The guard was inspected by Brig. J. Whitehead, C.B., C.M.G., C.B.E., D.S.O., and Col. Brook. On the last occasion, November 11, 1944, the guard was formed up in Broad Sanctuary for inspection by Col. Brook, accompanied by Major H. Cowan, O.C. of No. 1 Coy., 1st London (Westminster) Batt.

Grace Goldin's painting *Home Guard Vigil* was presented to Major H. Cowan's company by the mother of one of his officers.

The battalion stand-down parade was held on Sunday, December 3. They mustered at Turnham Green and attended service at the Parish Church. The band accompanied the service which, as usual, was conducted by the padre, the Rev. S. Osborne-Goodchild, A.K.S. The battalion then marched to Brentford and Chiswick Town Hall, where they were addressed by the Deputy Director-General Home Guard, Brig. J. A. Longmore, M.B.E., T.D., Col. Brook, the Mayor (Alderman T. W. Stroud, J.P.) and the C.O. The expressions of appreciation by the various speakers left no doubt that the services of all had been invaluable to the nation and an example to future generations. An appreciation of the C.O. was expressed by Sgt. E. C. Taylor, of H.Q. Coy., who spoke for all ranks.

The following honours and awards were received by members of the battalion : Lieut. Col. H. K. Cleary, O.B.E. ; Sgt. S. W. Chambers, B.E.M. ; Cpl. G. W. McCarty, Commendation by G.O.C. in London District Orders ; and Capt. F. C. Rainbird, C.Q.M.S. S. E. Ware, C.S.M. H. W. Sanders, Sgt. E. L. Ingram, Sgt. J. Moss, Sgt. H. G. Ruane, Sgt. W. G. Bambrough, Sgt. G. Andrews, Sgt. E. D. Read, Sgt. G. Cole, Sgt. R. A. H. Hall, Sgt. A. J. Hans, Sgt. R. G. Seagrave, Sgt. W. S. Hobden, Cpl. A. S. Parfitt, Cpl. A. Rollo, L/Cpl. A. Wilcox and Pte. L. H. Davies, Certificates of Merit.

ROLL OF OFFICERS AT 'STAND DOWN'

Name and Rank	*Appointment*
Battalion Headquarters	
Lieut. Col. H. K. Cleary, O.B.E.	Officer Commanding
Major E. D. Peaty	Second-in-Command
Major J. L. Thomas	Battalion Medical Officer
Capt. R. S. Gardner	Liaison Officer
Capt. F. C. Rainbird	Ammunition Officer
Capt. H. J. O'Mara	W.T. Officer
Capt. I. Andrew	Asst. Quartermaster
Lieut. S. J. Hubbard	Transport Officer
Lieut. J. B. Bennie	Camouflage Officer
Lieut. N. F. Bartlett	Gas Officer
Lieut. A. Barnes	Intelligence Officer
Lieut. G. T. Goulding	Signals Officer
Lieut. J. S. Laurie	P.A.D. Officer
Lieut. F. W. Bird	P.P.D. Officer
Lieut. A. E. Ashcroft	Asst. Adjutant and Bandmaster
Lieut. W. A. Salisbury	Bombing Officer
Lieut. S. G. W. Beacon	Pioneer Officer
Lieut. G. H. Mann	P.T. Officer
Lieut. G. W. Mathews	A.B.D. Officer
Capt. E. J. S. Davies (East Surrey Regt.)—Adjutant	

H.Q. Company	
Major F. D. Rose	Company Commander
Capt. A. S. Parfit	Second-in-Command
Lieut. W. J. Reading	O.C., No. 18 Platoon
Lieut. L. T. Ware	O.C., No. 19 Platoon
Lieut. H. G. Ruane	O.C., No. 20 Platoon
Lieut. S. Buckingham	O.C., No. 21 Platoon
2nd Lt. C. V. Taylor	Platoon Officer, No. 18 Platoon
2nd Lt. E. Goodyear	Platoon Officer, No. 20 Platoon
2nd Lt. F. E. Darling	Platoon Officer, No. 21 Platoon

A Company	
Major J. W. Ayris	Company Commander
Capt. E. M. Price	Second-in-Command
Lieut. A. T. Smith	O.C., No. 1 Platoon
Lieut. W. J. Sibley	Platoon Officer, No. 1 Platoon
Lieut. A. Shurey	O.C., No. 2 Platoon
Lieut. H. Harrup	Platoon Officer, No. 2 Platoon
Lieut. H. J. Barnard	O.C., No. 3 Platoon
Lieut. G. A. Osborne	O.C., No. 4 Platoon
Lieut. G. R. Allridge	Platoon Officer, No. 4 Platoon
2nd Lt. C. W. M. Coughlan	Platoon Officer, No. 3 Platoon

Name and Rank	*Appointment*
B Company	
Major A. V. Bond	Company Commander
Capt. W. Tarling	Second-in-Command
Lieut. G. Harper	O.C., No. 5 Platoon
Lieut. A. F. Manton	O.C., No. 6 Platoon
Lieut. W. Snelling, M.M.	O.C., No. 7 Platoon
Lieut. G. H. Crowfoot	O.C., No. 8 Platoon
2nd Lt. J. E. Lowe	Platoon Officer, No. 5 Platoon
2nd Lt. M. P. S. Allen	Platoon Officer, No. 6 Platoon
C Company	
Major J. Cracknell	Company Commander
Capt. R. Houlgrave	Second-in-Command
Lieut. W. F. Cook	O.C., No. 9 Platoon
Lieut. F. W. Keefe, M.M.	Platoon Officer, No. 9 Platoon
Lieut. A. T. Storey	O.C., No. 10 Platoon
Lieut. W. G. Hornsey	O.C., No. 11 Platoon
Lieut. F. W. Abbey	O.C., No. 12 Platoon
2nd Lt. E. L. Ingram	Platoon Officer, No. 10 Platoon
2nd Lt. R. E. H. Vincent	Platoon Officer, No. 11 Platoon
2nd Lt. I. E. Hersey	Platoon Officer, No. 12 Platoon
D Company	
Major G. G. Fisher	Company Commander
Capt. S. J. Creasey	Second-in-Command
Lieut. W. G. Braham	Platoon Officer, No. 13 Platoon
Lieut. F. T. Scutt	O.C., No. 14 Platoon
Lieut. W. H. Marritt	Platoon Officer, No. 14 Platoon
Lieut. D. O'Neill	O.C., No. 15 Platoon
Lieut. L. Davis	Platoon Officer, No. 16 Platoon
Lieut. S. E. Ware	O.C., No. 17 Platoon
2nd Lt. B. D. Baker	Platoon Officer, No. 13 Platoon
2nd Lt. H. G. Fry	Platoon Officer, No. 14 Platoon
2nd Lt. E. Fell	Platoon Officer, No. 15 Platoon
2nd Lt. R. W. Whit	Platoon Officer, No. 17 Platoon
Deceased	
Lieut. H. W. Webb	D Company
Lieut. L. J. Manwaring	D Company
Lieut. W. C. Rose, M.M.	D Company

9 The 44th Battalion

ORIGINALLY the 44th was the 4th Batt. and then had three companies made up from 31 bus garages, both central and country, south of the Thames, with battalion headquarters at A Central Bus Divisional office, Warner Road, Camberwell. The battalion area included Tunbridge Wells, Guildford, Windsor, Gravesend and other outlying garages. Each garage had its own platoon and the great Chiswick works formed a complete company—C Coy.

The Battalion Commander in the beginning was Major T. H. Powell, who, with Captain Buchanan, Battalion Adjutant, had been for many years in the King's Royal Rifle Corps. It was to this regiment that all L.P.T.B. Home Guards were affiliated, and the 44th proudly wore the K.R.R.C. badge.

Early Company Commanders were : A Coy., 16 garages, Mr. C. F. Ayres ; B Coy., 15 garages, Mr. H. Stanton ; and C Coy., Chiswick Works, Mr. G. H. Gillman.

Major Powell, Batt. C.O., became a Lieut. Col. when Home Guard officers were given commissions, and Major E. A. Tolchard was appointed his 2 i/c. The company commanders received the rank of Major, but, unfortunately, before this time, Mr. Stanton was forced to resign because of ill-health, and his place as Commander of B Coy. was taken by Mr. (later Major) L. Bicheno.

The battalion was re-designated the 44th County of London (L.P.T.B.) Batt. in March 1941. The increase to seven battalions in the following November and the consequent reorganisation did not cause such extensive changes as in most other units.

The battalion was re-constituted as follows:

LIEUTENANT-COLONEL T. H. POWELL AND SENIOR OFFICERS OF THE 44TH

A Company			
Coy. H.Q.	No 1 Platoon	(Camberwell Bus Garage)	
Camberwell	No. 2 Platoon	(Camberwell Tram Depot)—which had formerly furnished Nos. 2 & 3 Platoons of the 4th Batt.	
	No. 4 Platoon	(Old Kent Road Bus Garage)	
	No. 5 Platoon	(New Cross Tram Depot)	
	No. 6 Platoon	(Clapham Tram Depot)	
	No. 7 Platoon	(Surrey Docks Station)	

B Company		
Coy. H.Q.	No. 8 Platoon	(Plumstead Bus Garage)
Greenwich	No. 9 Platoon	(Sidcup Bus Garage)
Power House	No. 10 Platoon	(Abbey Wood Tram Depot)
	No. 11 Platoon	(Bexley Heath Trolleybus Depot)
	No. 12 Platoon	(Charlton Central Repair Depot)
	No. 13 Platoon	(Greenwich Power Station)

C Company		
Coy. H.Q.	No. 14 Platoon	(Nunhead Bus Garage)
65 Plaistow	No. 15 Platoon	(Elmers End Bus Garage)
Lane, Bromley	No. 16 Platoon	(Catford Bus Garage)
	No. 17 Platoon	(Bromley Bus Garage)

D Company		
Coy. H.Q.	No. 18 Platoon	(Northfleet Country Bus Garage)
Northfleet	No. 19 Platoon	(Dartford Country Bus Garage)
Country Bus	No. 20 Platoon	(Dunton Green Country Bus Garage)
Garage	No. 21 Platoon	(Tunbridge Wells Country Bus Garage)
	No. 22 Platoon	(Swanley Country Bus Garage)

The battalion retained this organisation for the rest of its life. None of the four companies retained the same commander for the whole period. Major Gordon (District Inspector, trams), first Commander of A Coy., had to retire because of pressure of civilian employment, and was succeeded by Major C. Ward (conductor, trams), full time. Capt. Gordon continued as 2 i/c.

B Coy. was originally commanded by Major Terry, who, by reason of pressure of work at the central repair depot, was unable to continue in the Home Guard and was succeeded by Major W. Wood (tool storekeeper, Greenwich Power Station). His 2 i/c was Capt. C. Coleman (Central bus conductor), full time.

Pressure of work also caused the retirement of Major L. Bicheno, who was succeeded by Major A. Hunt (staff allocation clerk, A divisional office, Central buses), formerly 2 i/c. Capt. C. Jennings (Central bus conductor) became 2 i/c, full time.

Major Ayres, D Coy., had to leave the Home Guard when appointed Temporary Deputy Regional Traffic Commissioner in Wales, and his 2 i/c, Capt. Henton, could not continue for private reasons. Major W. Kirshner (District engineer, country buses), formerly a platoon commander, took over command, with Capt. Fincham (country bus driver) as his 2 i/c, full time. The latter, in turn, had to relinquish 2 i/c of the company on being promoted to inspector, his place being taken by Capt. F. Wyles (country bus driver).

The battalion's first Quartermaster was Capt. J. Baxter (electrical foreman, A division, Central buses) who had the formidable task of equipping a battalion over 3,000 strong from scratch, working part-time only. No praise can be too high for his zeal, an opinion emphatically expressed by Capt. W. Mudford, Queen's Royal Regt., who succeeded him as full-time regular Quartermaster. The fact that it was concluded that regular full-time Quartermasters were necessary for Home Guard battalions is an indication of the work part-time Quartermasters undertook in the early days.

Upon the appointment of Capt. Mudford, Capt. Baxter reverted, by his own desire, to lieutenant and continued as Assistant Quartermaster. Capt. Mudford has expressed doubt as to whether he could have functioned effectively, certainly during the first few months, without Capt. Baxter's wholehearted assistance.

In November 1945, Capt. A. Buchanan, who had been gazetted as regular full-time Adjutant, was invalided from the Service and was succeeded by Capt. H. E. Adamson, King's Own Scottish Borderers, who remained as Adjutant until the Home Guard Adjutants were withdrawn.

Dr. Guy Bousfield, bacteriologist to the boroughs of Camberwell, Hackney and Wandsworth, became the battalion's first Medical Officer, with the rank of Major. The initial medical organisation and training of the battalion fell to him, and entailed a great amount of work. Dr. A. C. White Knox, M.C., Dr. A. Riddell and Dr. T. C. Outred were subsequent medical officers. At his own request, Dr. Bousfield relinquished his appointment and majority in favour of Major White Knox, M.C., and became Capt. and Medical Officer to B Coy., Capt. Riddell being Medical Officer to C Coy. and Capt. Outred to D Coy. Major White Knox was responsible for the general medical arrangements and training of the battalion, plus medical charge of A Coy. The battalion was fortunate in having Dr. White Knox, who for many years had been associated with the St. John Ambulance Brigade, of which he was a deputy commissioner.

Other Specialist Officers were :

Weapon Training Officer—Capt. J. McKeown (conductor, Camberwell buses), who formerly served in the K.R.R.C. and was an exceptionally fine shot and very active in S.M.R.C. circles.

Ammunition Officer—Capt. J. Reilley (driver, Camberwell buses), who unfortunately was compelled to leave the Home Guard on account of ill-health. He was succeeded by Capt. H. Dix (inspector Central buses), who, in addition, conducted a class in map reading, in which he had been trained at the

Royal Air Force aerodrome, Biggin Hill. He was also Catering Officer and functioned most successfully in field exercises and social events.

Security and Intelligence Officer — the first was Capt. Leslie Williams, M.B.E., a partner of Messrs. Hitchcock Williams, textile merchants, of St. Paul's Churchyard, City. He had, during the 1914-18 war, been engaged in the suppression of the drug traffic across the Red Sea, and was Political Officer and Commander of the Desert Police in Mesopotamia. He subsequently became Liaison Officer and his place was taken by Lieut. Long (plans office, 55, Broadway).

Bombing Officer—Lieut. J. Broderick (driver, Nunhead bus garage).

Passive Air Defence Officer—Lieut. L. Read (divisional foreman, A division, Central buses), until pressure of work in connection with gas-producer buses made it impossible for him to continue, and his place was taken by Lieut. H. Staton (night foreman, Catford bus garage), one of London Transport's A.R.P. instructors.

Signals Officer—Lieut. C. Payne (driver, Camberwell bus garage), who organised and trained, with the assistance of his N.C.O.s, an enthusiastic and efficient Signals section. They equipped themselves at their own expense, using their own ingenuity. Latterly, it was possible to allocate a portion of the training grant for this purpose.

Physical Training, Unarmed Combat and Street Fighting Officer—Lieut A. Sharman, O.B.E. (driver, Camberwell tram depot), although over 40 took the street-fighting course with the Regular Army at Battersea and did so well that a special letter of commendation was received by the sub-district commander from the commandant of the school, a Guards officer.

Camouflage Officer—Lieut. W. Burden (clerk, Camberwell tram depot). In addition to assisting extensively with the administration of A Coy., Lieut. Burden undertook the duties of Camouflage Officer, in which he was extremely fortunate in his assistant, Sgt.

Milne, whose wife made outstanding equipment and apparatus.

Transport Officer—Lieut. P. Mumford (dock foreman, Camberwell bus garage), devoted much time and skill to keeping battalion transport operationally efficient.

Petrol Disruption Officer—Lieut. A. W. Fincham (inspector country services), who had previously been Sgt. Major and subsequently 2 i/c of D Coy., was compelled to take a less active part in Home Guard work on promotion from driver to inspector and became Petrol Disruption Officer in succession to Lieut. Dix when the latter became Ammunition Officer.

O.C. M.T. Detachment—Lieut. J. Edwards (Dunlop tyre fitter, Camberwell bus garage).

Assistant Adjutant—nominally, Lieut. H. Rawlings (inspector, trams).

When the Army Council sanctioned honorary chaplains, the Rev. Anthony Toller, St. Giles, Camberwell, undertook the duties for the battalion. Padre Toller, tall, athletic, extremely human and approachable, and with a grand sense of humour, travelled about the battalion area on a somewhat ancient motor cycle, which always seemed a little too small for him, and soon became widely known and extremely popular. So far as his parochial duties and the large battalion area permitted, he took part in all activities, holding periodical parade services in St. Giles Church, conducting funerals and weddings, attending field exercises and social functions, shooting on the range and, on occasion, peeling potatoes. His addresses at parade services will always be remembered. His sermons were direct, topical and not without humour, and were delivered with an earnestness and understanding which were understood and appreciated by even the toughest men. Battalion church parades were always strongly attended and no comments were ever heard to the effect that they were unnecessary. On the Home Guard standing down the battalion's opinion of Padre Toller was conveyed to his bishop.

He continued as chaplain to the battalion of the Army Cadet Force, and became vicar of St. George's Church, Perry Hill, Catford. The battalion was represented at his induction.

Training began when the L.D.V. was formed. Before the battalion came into being guards were mounted at all platoon headquarters. The amount of sheer hard work put in by all ranks during the battalion's five years' existence was amply demonstrated. As always, the spade work fell upon platoon commanders, platoon officers and N.C.O.s, who, for a long period in the beginning, without weapons or equipment, sweated at the apparently hopeless task of preparing to meet probable German invasion. Improvisation of every description was resorted to, such as dummy rifles and grenades, and numerous aids to training were devised and made by the platoons themselves.

Gradually weapons were issued, the training at once became more interesting, and enthusiasm increased.

Rifles and bayonets, automatic weapons, and various forms of sub-artillery, such as the Smith gun, Spigot mortar, two-pound anti-tank gun, Browning, together with 'kosh', and the always-to-be-remembered pike, came along, and after rather more than two years the battalion reached its maximum in equipment. No one ventured to issue a pike to an individual member of the battalion, and it remained a closely guarded 'secret weapon'.

Many officers and men attended courses at the War Office schools and training centres, such as No. 1 G.H.Q. Home Guard School at Denbies, near Dorking, the South-Eastern Command Weapon Training School, street-fighting courses at Battersea and Birmingham, gas course, fieldcraft school at Burwash, school of cookery, weapon school, Purfleet, etc., while R.S.M. Ingram and others were attached for a week to a battalion of the Scots Guards undergoing field training in Wales. Other officers and N.C.O.s were attached to Regular Army battalions for a time, and good reports were invariably received.

Training went on busily in the evenings

THE 44TH BATTALION AND BAND

and at week-ends. Field training and battle drill, route marches, camouflage and field-craft, musketry (both miniature and full-bore), bombing, Smith gun, Spigot mortar, field cooking, and map reading were all taught.

Exercises in the open were carried out whenever possible, and in winter halls were hired for indoor training.

The Signals section carried out numerous exercises, both by day and night, and in open country, on an ambitious scale, combining them with field cooking. They also installed communication between certain platoons and operational sites, such as the defensive positions of an anti-aircraft battery, as well as inter-communication between the various posts in Greenwich Power Station—a V.P. for which the battalion was responsible. They made practical use of almost all methods of signalling with the exception of wireless, i.e. land lines (both morse and telephone), flags and lamp signalling (both night and daylight). Training in field W.T. was also carried out with such few sets as were available, and a considerable proportion of the officers of the battalion were instructed in W.T. procedure.

The battalion was fortunate in having the use of a cinematograph for showing training films. Pte. Barton, assistant mechanical engineer (Underground railways), who was later promoted lieutenant and Unit Signals Officer, placed his full-size projector at the battalion's disposal, and this was installed at Flanders Barracks, Flodden Road, Camberwell.

Batt. Pioneer Sgt. Mayer, who had previous experience of cinematograph operation, became Lieut. Barton's assistant, and together they spent a great part of their leisure in adding to and perfecting their apparatus and constructing a second projector, and many training films were shown to the 44th and their neighbours, the 13th and 14th Batts., while Sgt. Mayer, with a 16 mm. projector of his own, showed enter-

tainment films to the families of members of all three battalions.

The battalion sent detachments to the unit week-end training camps at Barnes, and later Stanmore, whenever duties permitted, and B Coy. held week-end camps and exercises at Sidcup on the platoon's training ground.

The 13th Batt. placed Flanders Barracks at the disposal of the battalion, which was most useful for A Coy. and battalion head-quarters training, and the officers and sergeants of the 44th were made honorary members of the respective messes. The battalion was indebted to Col. Hill, the Commanding Officer, for this courtesy.

Other barracks which were placed at the battalion's disposal were Artillery House, Catford, by the courtesy of the O.C., 57th London Batt., and Watling Street Barracks, Bexley, by the courtesy of the O.C., 56th Kent Batt. The miniature ranges at both these barracks were particularly useful to the battalion, as were others placed at our disposal by other units. The battalion had ranges of its own at Sidcup, Plumstead, Charlton works and New Cross, the three latter being constructed by the platoons themselves. New Cross and Sidcup also constructed their own assault courses. Full-bore shooting took place at Bisley, Milton (near Gravesend), Shoreham (near Farning-ham) and Tunbridge Wells, also Plumstead, and on the L.M.S. range at Battersea, and the majority of the battalion completed the war course. Bombing practice was carried out at Surrey Docks, Sidcup, Bickley and Dartford, the first on a specially constructed range and the others in adapted quarries and sandpits. Smith gun and Spigot mortar practice took place on the marshes near Belvedere.

Three permanent staff instructors served with the battalion—Sgt. McCallum, London Scottish ; Sgt. Day, Royal West Kents ; and Sgt. Jones, K.R.R.C. The first was returned to his unit, but the others stayed with the battalion to the end.

The battalion had a training library, thanks to material presented by Capt. Williams. At stand down the bulk of this library was passed to the Army Cadet Force.

It is a tribute to the battalion that several letters were received from some of the younger men who were called up for the Services, saying how valuable they had found the training, and in some cases it had resulted in early promotion.

Haste and intensiveness of training in the emergency meant some accidents, and the battalion had its share. Fortunately, only one was really serious, this being caused by the premature explosion of a No. 68 grenade, which wounded fourteen. Most of the injuries were slight, but among the more seriously hurt was Lieut. Pennells, D.C.M., who was over 60, a veteran of the South African War, and had also had his home destroyed. Happily, he made a good recovery, as did the others.

Because of the large area covered by the battalion, it was impossible for it to undertake an operational role as such, so that, while still being administered as a homogeneous unit, each platoon was under the operational command of the local battalion nearest to it. In the majority of cases this arrangement proved satisfactory. In some cases the platoon became part of the general reserve of the local battalion; in others it was given the defence of a particular locality, and in others it formed a counter-attacking force, with a predetermined and important task. The Greenwich platoon was responsible for the power station, an important V.P., and Charlton works with the defence of the factory. The Bromley platoon, under Capt. Jennings, formed a mobile platoon and was responsible for containing Sundridge Park golf course should parachutists land there, while the Sidcup platoon, under Capt. Gifford, was given a similar role. For a time the Sidcup platoon undertook the combat training of the R.A.P.C. unit stationed there, which received instruction on the assault course and miniature anti-tank gun range which the platoon had constructed, as well as on the miniature range. The Abbey Wood platoon was responsible for the protection of the local A.A. battery.

Some platoons also did subsidiary work. Northfleet platoon formed a bomb disposal section ; the medical personnel of New Cross platoon, under Sgt. Burroughs, manned a Borough of Deptford first-aid vehicle during the entire flying-bomb period. This platoon had a most efficient first-aid section.

Another of the duties undertaken throughout the war was mine watching at Greenwich power house. A Royal Navy launch, often H.M.S. *Water Gipsy*, commanded by Petty Officer Sir A. P. Herbert, towed a small balloon up and down the Thames at night and periodically one of the crew illuminated it with an Aldis lamp for ten seconds at predetermined spots. This simulated a parachute mine about to drop into the river and the watchers at Greenwich, and many other places, had to plot the positions and send them, together with the times, to the Flag Officer, Port of London, at Tower Bridge. Those sent in by Greenwich were of a consistently high degree of accuracy and earned the flag officer's praise.

Immediately before and after D Day it was thought that there would be paratroop raids on industries and plants vital to the prosecution of the war, and the guard at Greenwich power station, which had been discontinued some time before when guards at platoon and company H.Q. were stopped, was re-introduced. All battalions, other than those widely distributed like this one, were ordered to have 200 officers and men under arms each night in case of a surprise attack, but in spite of the exemption, Bromley furnished a complete platoon of 36 for this duty one night each month.

Many times members of the battalion turned out to help the A.R.P. authorities in rescue work. In anticipation of heavy bombing during the D Day period, a percentage of each platoon was trained by the local A.R.P. in light rescue work.

Thirty-three women joined the battalion as auxiliaries and the work they did varied. Some had more opportunities, some fewer, but the battalion were grateful for their help and it was satisfactory to know that they were ready, should the Home Guard have gone into action. Many took the St. John Ambulance course and qualified in first-aid. One woman was so enthusiastic that she provided herself with a service-dress uniform, complete with shoulder titles and flashes, and appeared at a church parade at which the brigadier took the salute and Col. Brook was present.

As the Directorate had just issued positive orders that women auxiliaries were not to wear uniform, this was not one of the commanding officer's best moments ! This splendid woman (of whose effort he privately entirely approved) would possibly have escaped notice had she not turned to the right when her platoon was ordered to turn left. The brigadier and unit commander were most helpful, however, and after their initial astonishment, assured the C.O. that they had not seen her. Measures were taken, however, to ensure that the photograph in which she was shown did not fall into the hands of the Press.

Miss M. Breaman, the first to join, carried out the duties of assistant adjutant during the whole of the battalion's existence, typing 90 per cent of the headquarter's communications. She is now assistant secretary of the Old Comrades' Association.

It has been stated that battalion church parades were held, but mention must be made of one in particular, that on Armistice Sunday, 1942, when Col. John Morrow, Jr., of the U.S. Army, who in civil life was then Vice-President of the International Harvester Company, Chicago, was the battalion's guest. He inspected and addressed the battalion at Flanders Barracks, presented a Good Service Certificate, then went to the parade service and took the salute as the battalion marched back, afterwards being the guest of the battalion in the mess. He expressed himself as very gratified at being the battalion's guest, and in November 1944, in the course of addressing the Harvesters Club in Chicago, he said, 'I would like to say a word about the British Home Guard. It was organised for the defence of the homeland, in case the Germans attempted an invasion. It was composed of older men, fit, but too old or unequal to the strenuous life of the Regular Army which was being sent overseas. They were drawn from many walks of life, all gainfully employed in essential industries and public services, many of them veterans of the last war. They did their training after working hours. Invited by its commander, I had the opportunity of inspecting a battalion of the Home Guard located just outside London (Camberwell ?) at their Armistice Day ceremonies. They were well trained and well equipped, and were to be congratulated on their discipline and efficiency. Prior to the inspection I was asked to present to one of the members a citation for bravery and devotion to duty during air raids. I felt quite honoured to make this presentation.'

The battalion was a very sociable one, and many concerts, dinners and dances were held by platoons in all companies. On two occasions as many officers of the battalion as civil duties permitted dined together, on the first occasion at the 'Bridge House', London Bridge, and on the second at battalion headquarters, when Col. Brook was their guest. These two dinners were most successful functions and were the nearest the battalion got to a regimental mess. Unfortunately, the large area—450 square miles—covered by the battalion, and the shift system of civil duty, made the formation of one impossible, to the regret of all officers.

Two sports meetings were held, one in 1942 by A Coy. in aid of the battalion's Prisoners of War Fund, and a battalion meeting in

1943, both at the sports ground at Bellingham. Prizes were presented by the C.O. and various members of the battalion.

In 1942 an assault at arms between the battalion and the 14th Batt. was held at Flanders Barracks, the sub-district and zone commanders being present, together with a large audience from both battalions. Competitions in miniature musketry, grenade throwing, stripping and assembling the tommy-gun, and drill were held, the 14th winning handsomely.

One of the battalion's notable activities was its Prisoners of War Fund. In the early days Major Tolchard suggested to company and platoon commanders that, as the battalion wore the badge of the King's Royal Rifle Corps, it would be a tribute to the corps to do something for its prisoners. The suggestion was enthusiastically received and the response was, to quote Major-Gen. J. Hare, C.B., D.S.O., a member of the corps, 'magnificent'.

When the fund was finally wound up it amounted to £1,500, the Old Kent Road platoon topping the list with £362 13s. 2d. Many letters of appreciation were received from the corps and published in battalion orders, and the Senior Col. Commandant, . Major-Gen. Sir John Davidson, C.B., K.C.M.G., D.S.O., personally expressed to the commanding officer at a meeting of the senior officers of the corps its thanks for the battalion's generous help.

The 'Geary' Cup was presented by Mr. S. R. Geary (operating manager, Central buses), to be competed for by platoons each half year. This was won by the Camberwell tram platoon on the first two occasions, and by Sidcup platoon on the third. L/Cpl. Plumpton and Pte. Foy of No. 8 (Plumstead) platoon each presented a cup for platoon competition.

Mr. Bicheno (divisional engineer, A division, Central buses) also presented a cup to be similarly competed for. One competition took place, the cup being won by Camberwell tram platoon. Capt. Adamson, the Adjutant, presented a handsome cup

to be shot for by all ranks of the battalion, full-bore rifle, at Bisley, and won outright. Some 85 officers, N.C.O.s and men competed and after a very keen competition and a tie between Pte. Burns, New Cross platoon, and Cpl. Palmer, Plumstead platoon, the cup was won by the latter.

The following members of the battalion were awarded Certificates of Merit :

R.S.M. O. Ingram, Headquarters
Sgt. F. Juniper, No. 13 Platoon
Sgt. A. F. Burroughs, No. 5 Platoon
Sgt. G. Milne, Headquarters
Cpl. F. A. Greenaway, No. 22 Platoon
Sgt. F. R. Pautard, Headquarters
Pte. A. E. Bristow, No. 1 Platoon

The stand-down parade and final gathering of the battalion was a great event. Plans were for the battalion to parade at Myatts Fields, Camberwell, at 4.0 p.m. for inspection by Brig. John Moubray, D.S.O., Scots Guards, commanding south-east London sub-district, afterwards addressing the battalion and present a Good Service Certificate to L/Cpl. Juniper of No. 13 Platoon, B Coy., for services rendered during a heavy air raid.

The battalion were then to march to St. Giles' Church for a short service, conducted by the Chaplain, the Rev. Anthony Toller, the salute being taken en route by the brigadier, accompanied by Col. Brook and the Mayor of Camberwell, Councillor H. Round. After the service there was to have been an informal social with refreshments and the presentation of cups for shooting at St. Giles' Hall. The weather, unfortunately, was so bad that the programme had to be altered.

The battalion—58 officers and 300 other ranks, plus the band—had just fallen in when the rain started, and ended with a cloud-burst at the moment of the brigadier's arrival, with the commander, at 4.0 p.m. For all the effect it had on the parade, however, the sun might have been shining. The rain ran off noses and chins, down necks and into eyes, boots and the commanding officer's beard, but the steadiness of the parade was complete.

ROLL OF OFFICERS AT 'STAND DOWN'

Name and Rank	*Appointment*
Battalion Headquarters	
Lieut. Col. T. H. Powell	Officer Commanding
Major E. A. Tolchard	Second-in-Command
Major A. C. White Knox, M.C.	Battalion Medical Officer
Capt. J. McKeown	Weapon Training Officer
Capt. L. Williams, M.B.E.	Liaison Officer
Capt. H. Dix	Ammunition Officer
Capt. W. Fincham	Petrol Disruption Officer
Lieut. J. Baxter	Assistant Adjutant
Lieut. C. Payne	Signals Officer
Lieut. W. Burdon	Camouflage Officer
Lieut. A. Sharman, O.B.E.	P.T. Officer
Lieut. J. Broderick	Bombing Officer
Lieut. H. Rawlings	Assistant Adjutant
Lieut. E. Long	Intelligence and Security Officer
Lieut. P. Mumford	Transport Officer
Lieut. H. Staton	P.A.D. Officer
Lieut. J. Edwards	O.C., M.T. Detachment
2nd Lt. T. Jupp	Assistant Signals Officer
Capt. H. E. Adamson, K.O.S.B.	Adjutant
Capt. W. Mudford, Q.R.R.	Quartermaster
A Company	
Major C. Ward	Company Commander
Capt. A. Gordon	Second-in-Command
Capt. G. Bousfield	Medical Officer
Lieut. G. Whittington	O.C., No. 1 Platoon
Lieut. G. Stokes	O.C., No. 2 Platoon
Lieut. G. Shirley	O.C., No. 4 Platoon
Lieut. R. Brooker, M.M.	O.C., No. 5 Platoon
Lieut. S. Thompsett	Platoon Officer, No. 5 Platoon
Lieut. H. Boyce	Platoon Officer, No. 2 Platoon
Lieut. A. Sinclair	O.C., No. 6 Platoon
Lieut. W. Buse	O.C., No. 7 Platoon
Lieut. H. Taylor	O.C., No. 6 Platoon (seconded to the Army)
2nd Lt. C. Dennison	Platoon Officer, No 2 Platoon (Cadet Force)
2nd Lt. O'Donoghue	Platoon Officer, No. 7 Platoon
2nd Lt. R. Wightwick	Platoon Officer, No. 4 Platoon
2nd Lt. S. Shilling	Platoon Officer, No. 5 Platoon
2nd Lt. W. Brown	Platoon Officer, No. 6 Platoon
2nd Lt. H. Jones	Platoon Officer, No. 6 Platoon
2nd Lt. F. Towersey	Platoon Officer, No. 1 Platoon

Name and Rank	*Appointment*
B Company	
Major W. Wood	Company Commander
Capt. C. Coleman	Second-in-Command
Capt. B. Gifford	O.C., No. 9 Platoon
Lieut. A. Johnson	O.C., No. 13 Platoon
Lieut. G. Watson	Platoon Officer, No. 9 Platoon
Lieut. A. Buckley	O.C., No. 11 Platoon
Lieut. G. Harris	O.C., No. 12 Platoon
Lieut. W. Reeves	Platoon Officer, No. 13 Platoon
Lieut. S. Mould	Platoon Officer, No. 11 Platoon
Lieut. T. Stone	O.C., No. 8 Platoon
Lieut. W. Cridland	O.C., No. 10 Platoon
2nd Lt. F. Butler	Platoon Officer, No. 8 Platoon
2nd Lt. J. McCombie	Platoon Officer, No. 9 Platoon
2nd Lt. J. Elliott	Platoon Officer, No. 9 Platoon
2nd Lt. A. Marks	Platoon Officer, No. 10 Platoon
2nd Lt. A. Booth	Platoon Officer, No. 12 Platoon
C Company	
Major A. Hunt	Company Commander
Capt. C. Jennings	Second-in-Command
Lieut. R. Piggott	Platoon Officer, No. 14 Platoon
Lieut. J. Jeffrey, M.M.	O.C., No. 15 Platoon
Lieut. C. Pennells, D.C.M.	Platoon Officer, No. 16 Platoon
Lieut. T. Shergold	O.C., No. 17 Platoon
2nd Lt. J. Edwards	Platoon Officer, No. 17 Platoon
2nd Lt. F. Allen	Platoon Officer, No. 17 Platoon
2nd Lt. W. Hyde	Platoon Officer, No. 15 Platoon
2nd Lt. H. Barrett	Platoon Officer, No. 16 Platoon
2nd Lt. G. Jones	Platoon Officer, No. 15 Platoon
Lieut. W. Boston	O.C., No. 14 Platoon
Lieut. W. Fudge	O.C., No. 16 Platoon
Capt. A. Riddell	Medical Officer
D Company	
Major W. Kirshner	Company Commander
Capt. E. Wyles	Second-in-Command
Capt. T. Outred	Medical Officer
Lieut. J. Gibson	O.C., No. 19 Platoon
Lieut. E. Grey	O.C., No. 21 Platoon
Lieut. A. Zealey	Platoon Officer, No. 20 Platoon
Lieut. P. Masters	Platoon Officer, No. 22 Platoon
Lieut. A. G. Lock	O.C., No. 18 Platoon
Lieut. L. Henry	O.C., No. 22 Platoon
Lieut. N. Preece	O.C., No. 20 Platoon
2nd Lt. R. Palmer	Platoon Officer, No. 19 Platoon
2nd Lt. C. Hawkes	Platoon Officer, No. 18 Platoon

Name and Rank	*Appointment*
Resigned, Transferred,	
or Honourably Discharged	
Capt. E. Reilly	Ammunition Officer
Lieut. L. Read	P.A.D. Officer
Lieut. W. Preston	Petrol Disruption Officer
Major H. Stanton	Company Commander, A Coy., 4th Batt.
Capt. E. Terry	Second-in-Command, B Coy.
Major L. Bicheno	Company Commander, C Coy.
2nd Lt. R. Holmes	Platoon Officer, No. 2 Platoon
Lieut. D. Durant	Platoon Officer, No. 4 Platoon
Lieut. W. Woodcock	O.C., No. 6 Platoon
Lieut. B. Hulyer	O.C., No. 8 Platoon
Lieut. A. Coomber	Platoon Officer, No. 8 Platoon
2nd Lt. H. Tyler	O.C., No. 10 Platoon
Lieut. C. Beeton	O.C., No. 10 Platoon
Lieut. T. Palmer	O.C., No. 11 Platoon
Lieut. W. Norman	O.C., No. 12 Platoon
Lieut. C. Bridges	O.C., No. 15 Platoon
Lieut. H. Carter	Platoon Officer, No. 17 Platoon
Lieut. J. Williams	Platoon Officer, No. 18 Platoon
Capt. W. Henton	Second-in-Command, D Coy.

Still serving with the Battalion in the Ranks, at own request

Pte. W. Beard	Platoon Officer, No. 1 Platoon
L/Cpl. F. Lesquesne	Platoon Commander, No. 1 Platoon
Pte. J. Crawford	Platoon Commander, No. 18 Platoon
Pte. F. Greenaway	Platoon Commander, No. 22 Platoon
Pte. F. Eatwell	Platoon Commander, No. 22 Platoon
Sgt. P. Brockman	Platoon Commander, No. 22 Platoon

Called up to Regular Forces

J. B. Dalton	Platoon Commander, No. 11 Platoon (killed as a result of motor-cycle accident in Italy)
T. Hollingdale	Platoon Commander, No. 18 Platoon
W. Cheeseman	Platoon Officer, Horwood Platoon (prior to reorganisation of 1941)

10 *The 45th Battalion*

THE staff of the tram and trolleybus departments of London Transport formed two L.D.V. battalions, the bulk of the 5th Batt. being obtained from men working south of the Thames. Mr. L. B. Hewitt, as Assistant Organiser, handled all earlier enrolments of both the 5th and 6th Batts. Their first headquarters were at Fulwell trolleybus depot, which, by June 1940, was controlling more than 2,000 men.

In August 1941 Mr. E. R. Alford, M.C., was selected battalion commander, and he received his rank as Lieut. Col. in the following February. At this time the headquarters moved to Hounslow trolleybus depot, the original premises at Fulwell being retained as Quartermaster's stores.

The organisation of the battalion was based on four companies, which, with the granting of commissions, were commanded by the following :

A Company	*B Company*
Major Braidwood	Major Gordon
C Company	*D Company*
Major A. F. Bentall	Major W. Wood

Owing to pressure of work Mr. Bentall resigned his C Coy. command in January 1941, and the company lost an understanding and efficient officer who had worked hard with the difficult tasks of the organisation of the early L.D.V. His 2 i/c, Mr. A. G. Drury, was promoted C Coy. Commander, and remained there until his promotion to battalion 2 i/c after the reorganisation.

The Quartermaster was Capt. L. R. Rogers, who was posted to the battalion in July 1941, followed some time later by Capt.

W. Leech, who was attached to the battalion as Adjutant.

The reorganisation in November 1941 left only two trolleybus depots and the Fulwell works in the battalion, the remaining strength being provided by units transferred from other battalions. In addition to controlling the nine central and country bus garages and three stations, the battalion now contained the Home Guard units of Acton works and Ealing Common and Northfields railway depots. The new organisation was as follows :

A Company
Major J. Schofield, M.C.
No. 1 Platoon. Fulwell
No. 2 Platoon. Twickenham Garage
No. 3 Platoon. Hounslow Depot
No. 4 Platoon. Hounslow Garage

B Company
Major E. W. Clark
No. 5 Platoon. Acton Town Station
No. 6 Platoon. Osterley Station
No. 7 Platoon. Hanwell Garage
No. 8 Platoon. Hanwell Depot

C Company
Major E. Major
No. 9 Platoon. Acton Works
No. 10 Platoon. Acton Works
No. 11 Platoon. Ealing Common Rly. Depot
No. 12 Platoon. Northfields Rly. Depot

D Company
Major W. G. Turner
No. 13 Platoon. Windsor Country Buses
No. 14 Platoon. Staines Country Buses
No. 15 Platoon. Addlestone Country Buses
No. 16 Platoon. Leatherhead Country Buses
No. 17 Platoon. Dorking Country Buses
No. 18 Platoon. Guildford Country Buses

No history of the 45th would be complete without reference to No. 1 platoon, A Coy., under the command of Major J. Schofield, M.C. Situated at Fulwell trolleybus depot, this platoon from the start showed great interest in shooting, which in time brought them recognition. After winning various matches, they entered for the S.M.R.C., Mackworth Praed Silver Challenge Cup in 1943. 1,554 teams entered from all parts of the country. In the first stage the 45th team, drawn from No. 1 platoon, scored 972 out of 1,000 and were placed 3rd for all England. Although they did not reach top position in the final stage, their achievement was most satisfactory for a team largely composed of shift workers shooting against stiff opposition. The following month they won a contest against the Hackney Rifle Club by 21 points, Hackney suffering their first defeat for five years. No. 1 platoon later won the return match as well—by three points. In the same year they entered a team in the N.R.A. Home Guard and Cadet Miniature Rifle Competition. L/Cpl. C. O. Oakham, by scoring a possible, obtained first place and a prize of life membership of the N.R.A.

Reorganisation gave the new B Coy. a unique mixture of Board's staff; C.M.E. railways, operating railways, signals department, permanent way, building, operating (buses), operating (trolleybuses), engineering (buses), engineering (trolleybuses). No better answer could have been given to those who were doubtful of the advisability of mixing staff from different branches of London Transport. From the start these men combined to form a team, of which their Company Commander, Major F. T. Muncey, later wrote, ' A truly representative London Transport team . . . I never hope to meet a better set of men.' This company was at first led by Major E. W. Clark, but owing to pressure of civilian work he relinquished his command in November 1942. Following the change of command, some adjustment was made to the organisation. Northfields Railway Depot, No. 12 platoon, C Coy., was transferred to B Coy. and became No. 5 platoon, whilst the original No. 5 platoon— Acton Town—was transferred to C Coy. and became No. 12 platoon. The largest portion of the company, that formed by Nos. 7 and 8 platoons—Hanwell bus and trolleybus staffs—provided General Service troops who were attached to the 10th Middlesex Batt. Home Guard in battle.

Their important operational role covered the area between the Great Western Railway and the Brent Canal on the outer defences of Heston Airport. No. 5 platoon was used entirely for the defence of Northfields depot, while No. 6 platoon—Osterley—came under the 2nd Middlesex Batt. for operations in the defence of the Great West Road. Much later, in 1944, No. 7 and 8 platoons were drawn into a ' defended locality ' around the Great Western Railway Hanwell viaduct.

Much of their training was centred around minor exercises, testing and improving their operational dispositions. Full 'Stand to' was tested on two night operations, during which all feeding and Q services operated fully, together with casualty clearing stations working in conjunction with V.A.D. detachments. As usual, the C.D. and N.F.S. were present to give valuable co-operation. During the major exercises, in which T sector attacked X sector, B Coy. encountered the 60th London L.P.T.B. in defence of Northolt aerodrome.

Before and after D Day B Coy. provided the inlying picket with the 10th Middlesex every night from April to July 1944. This made a very heavy call on the company, but all ranks responded splendidly. The keenness and efficiency of Capt. Budgeon as Coy. 2 i/c helped in this company's success, which resulted in their holding both battalion challenge cups in 1943.

C Coy., composed of four platoons, drew its men from Acton and Ealing Common works and from some members of the traffic and engineering departments staffs who had a platoon headquarters at Acton town station. Company headquarters were in Acton works. This company originally came into being in the L.D.V. days as A Coy. of the 42nd Batt. and was then recruited entirely from Acton works. The company, which originally contained a strength of 350, was led in the first instance by Mr. F. Hayes of the car body shop, Acton works, who was an ex-Sgt. of the Grenadier Guards. In those threatening days a substantial guard of 20

operated nightly in addition to Saturday afternoons and all day Sundays.

These early guards were not without their exciting moments. Three times the works received direct hits from sticks of H.E. bombs in addition to one oil bomb.

The guards quarters, owing to lack of other accommodation, was in the sports pavilion. While accommodation was ample, protection was nil. This was particularly emphasised when the pavilion was straddled by two bombs which wrecked the roof and all windows.

Mr. Hayes left Acton works to work in the aircraft industry early in 1941 and Mr. C. Major of the staff office, Broadway, at that time an N.C.O. in the 43rd Batt., was brought in as company commander.

Major Major set about his new duties with alacrity, appointing new platoon commanders and drawing up useful and attractive training schedules. A great believer in the power of the social side, he organised company dances, several of which were held at the Albert Stanley Institute, Hammersmith garage.

After the 1941 reorganisation the composition of the company was made up of troops from Acton works, Ealing Common works and Northfields depot. This Northfields platoon later passed to the command of B Coy., in exchange for which the Acton Town station platoon became attached to C Coy. The alteration was necessary to suit local military requirements. C Coy. now came within the operational area of the 7th Middlesex Batt. Home Guard, and from then on until the stand down, worked in close liaison with A Coy. of that battalion.

The introduction of a battalion efficiency competition in 1942 created interest throughout the battalion. C Coy.'s team, led by Lieut. Holland, at that time in command of No. 11 platoon, received concentrated training from specialised instructors and won the coveted challenge cup in September that year.

Towards the end of 1943 Major Major found it difficult to give as much time as he felt was his duty to C Coy. because of the increasing demands of his work in the staff office. He relinquished his command in early 1944 and was succeeded by Mr. W. O. R. Davies, chief clerk to the electrical department, who had served in World War I as an artilleryman.

The company worked well under its new leader on the lines laid down for the training of the Home Guard in the London area.

The approach of D Day brought more duties to this company, such as bigger guards, permanent manning of company headquarters' telephones and 'in-lying' pickets. These increased duties were instituted in April and lasted until just before stand down. No history of C Coy., however short, would be complete without reference to the Signals section which operated under

Sgt. Stone. The amount of work put in by this N.C.O. and his team was really prodigious. In addition to wiring the whole of Acton works, they succeeded in connecting to Acton town station and Ealing Common works and company headquarters. The signalmen made their own instruments for use at both company and platoon headquarters. After D Day there was a call for volunteers to help handle R.A.S.C. material required for the Normandy beachhead. C Coy. were particularly in evidence in answering this call for volunteers, and sent large fatigue parties to Greenford and Northolt depots.

Like its brother battalions, the 45th carried one scattered company in its country area. D Coy. recruited its men from the Green Line and country bus garages, from Staines and Windsor to Addlestone, Leatherhead and Dorking. Formed from the original B Coy. of the 44th Batt., D Coy., from the 1941 reorganisation, was commanded by Major W. G. Turner, with Capt. C. King as 2 i/c. Spread over an area of many miles in length and depth, there were many difficulties of administration, yet the company thrived thanks to the team spirit within each remote platoon and the unstinted efforts of officers and N.C.O.s.

LIEUTENANT-COLONEL E. R. ALFORD, M.C., WITH HIS SENIOR OFFICERS

They were fortunate in having near them such magnificent regular troops as the Canadian Black Watch. In company with the 6th Batt. Surrey Home Guard, D Coy. gratefully accepted the Canadians' offer to take part in an extensive training course in the evenings and week-ends for three weeks. This training was identified by a marked increase in Home Guard efficiency. Many good friends were made during these weeks and many Home Guards will always remember their Canadian tutors who taught so hard and who later fought so hard at Dieppe . . . good friendship which must ever remain a memory.

The steady improvement and modernisation of the company went on, but the geographical difficulties were so great that in May 1943 authority was given to split the company. D Coy., now smaller and more wieldy, came under the command of Capt. C. King, who was soon promoted Major. Lieut. J. Powell received his captaincy and became 2 i/c.

Throughout their life this company was fortunate in their constant liaison with first-class Regular troops in the Surrey area. The many opportunities to improve their skill by these associations were never missed and continued until stand down.

Hardworking N.C.O.s formed the backbone of these scattered sub-units who, in this instance, were ably led by C.S.M. W. Land. The headaches of arms and equipment were always carried smilingly by C.Q.M.S. W. G. Randall.

The new company formed by the division of D Coy. became E Coy. under the command of Major Turner. With headquarters at Windsor garage, the new and small company began a series of training programmes which were destined to give a standard of military bearing and efficiency even above that of the normal Home Guard sub-unit.

This training was, in no small measure, due to the efforts of the Coy. 2 i/c, Capt. H. G. Call, an ex-Guardsman whose contacts with the Windsor garrison proved invaluable to the company. By the help of Lieut. Col. G. M. Cornish, O.B.E., M.C., E Coy. were given facilities for regular training in the Guards training centre at Windsor Great Park. Although at times very arduous, it is not surprising that from this background emerged a highly efficient Home Guard fighting machine. The company normally carried a strength of 170. Morale was high throughout, attendances exceptionally good and all ranks kept constantly on their toes by the considerable competition of the local Windsor Home Guards, who were themselves similarly trained and a great credit to their famous town.

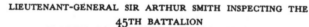

LIEUTENANT-GENERAL SIR ARTHUR SMITH INSPECTING THE
45TH BATTALION

Sixty-two members of E Coy. earned proficiency badges, while the whole company passed through the Regular Army battle inoculation course conducted by Sgt. Bren gunners of the Guards.

Two small field exercises were held each month under the guidance of Guards instructors. The defences of Windsor Castle were constantly tested by the joint action of the Home Guards in the vicinity and their tenacity caused more than one alteration to be made in the defences of this royal fortress.

Opportunities afforded by the Guards included exceptional facilities for full-bore musketry, while the Home Guard allocation of live grenades was always augmented by the Guards' training stock. It is not surprising that E Coy. boasted that almost any man could adequately fill any bomber's position in battle platoon.

Lieut. Gen. Sir Arthur Smith, as G.O.C. London District, visited the unit when training in Windsor Great Park and watched them at work, referring particularly to the quality of training given by Home Guard instructors and specially commended Sgt. Hunt on his bayonet-fighting instruction.

During the D Day period many volunteers were called for and many hours spent on special duties with the Guards. Their exceptional Home Guard life ended equally exceptionally. In view of their close association with the Windsor garrison, the King personally stood down the Windsor Home Guard in the grounds of Windsor Castle on December 10, 1944.

E Coy. sent every man whose duties would allow, including Major W. G. Turner, Capt. H. J. Call and Lieuts. Clark and Lampitt. His Majesty addressed the parade and after stressing the importance of the work they had done inspected the ranks and spoke to every man. The officers were later presented to the King and received personal thanks for their work.

Another increase in companies came in July 1944 when, in line with other Home Guard units, the 45th formed all specialist attachments into H.Q. Coy. under the command of Major A. E. P. Bawden. This six-company organisation continued unaltered until the stand down.

The two main competitions in the 45th Batt. were the contest for the battalion cup presented by the officers, and the Agnew cup presented by Mr. W. A. Agnew. The battalion cup provided an inter-company contest for the best company in foot and arms drill, turn-out and tactical training. First competed for in September 1942, the cup was won by C Coy. with 43 points, with A Coy. runners-up with 42½ points. The second contest, in May 1943, resulted in A Coy. again losing by half a point, this time B Coy. being the winners. A Coy. deservedly won the trophy at their third attempt in November 1943.

The Agnew Cup, also competed for on a company basis, was held by the best company at weapon training, including full-bore and miniature rifle, bombing, Northover and E.Y. rifle. B Coy. won this trophy when the first contest took place in June 1943.

The 45th were always well represented at all the Group anniversary parades. That in 1943 will always be remembered by the battalion. They were placed on the right of the parade and led the march past. Their fine bearing, good though it was, came below that of the Guard of Honour, also provided by the 45th Batt. This Guard of Honour, which received Lieut. Gen. Sir Arthur Smith, was the subject of discussion in Home Guard messes long after the parade, and fortunately was recorded for all time in the many photographs taken. It is one of the few regrets of the battalion that films were not made of these parades until the following year.

In the second parade before the King, on May 14, 1944, the battalion contingent formed part of the composite unit under the command of the Commanding Officer of the 53rd Surrey Home Guard Batt. After the parade this officer wrote, ' I should like to thank you for your co-operation and to congratulate you on the turnout of your detachment which formed part of F Batt. at the Home Guard parade on May 14. . . . I was honoured by having them under my command on such an important occasion.' During July 1944, A, B and C Coys. answered a call from the R.A.O.C. for assistance in packing equipment for Normandy. The response for volunteers was really magnificent and more than 700 working hours were given to this all-important, though heavy, work.

On Sunday, October 8, 1944, the 45th held their final battalion parade on Greenham Field, London Road, Isleworth. The Inspecting Officer, Brig. F. A. V. Copeland-Griffiths, D.S.O., M.C., and Col. E. T. Brook, C.B.E, addressed the parade after the inspection. To the music of the 43rd Batt. band, the battalion then marched past their C.O., Lieut. Col. E. R. Alford, M.C., and so marched away for the last time, except for the contingent which was provided for the official stand-down parade before the King in Hyde Park in December 1944. The following members of the battalion were awarded Certificates of Merit during the life of the battalion :

Cpl. J. L. Reynolds	C.S.M. J. C. Atlee
Cpl. A. C. Gurney	Sgt. F. A. Bonoor
Pte. L. J. Cotton	Lt. E. W. Humphries
Sgt. R. G. Stone	Sgt. W. Wigginton
Cpl. G. S. Spooner	Sgt. S. J. Butler
Cpl. J. Clowser	Sgt. J. W. Regardsoe
Pte. P. Upton	Sgt. A. S. Paine
Sgt. H. R. Tarrant	Sgt. F. G. Read
L/Cpl. J. R. Piggott	C/Sgt. T. H. Rees

ROLL OF OFFICERS AT 'STAND DOWN'

Name and Rank	Appointment
Battalion Headquarters	
Lieut. Col. E. R. Alford, M.C.	Officer Commanding
Major J. W. Harlock	Second-in-Command
Major M. G. Fitzgerald	Battalion Medical Officer
Capt. G. Brown	Liaison Officer
Capt. J. Eedle	Ammunition Officer
Capt. P. G. Norman	W.T. Officer
Capt. C. S. Colley	Asst. Quartermaster
Lieut. T. S. Allen	Camouflage Officer
Lieut. R. Rawkins	Gas Officer
Lieut. C. J. Pett	Intelligence Officer
Lieut. A. E. Rennie	Signals Officer
Lieut. F. C. French	P.A.D. Officer
Lieut. A. E. Courtenay	Asst. Adjutant
Lieut. R. Thomas	Bombing Officer
Lieut. E. C. Holland	Pioneer Officer
Lieut. D. Macomish	P.T. Officer
2nd Lt. T. W. Hodges	Transport Officer
2nd Lt. E. W. Humphries	Bomb Disposal
Capt. W. Leech	Adjutant
Capt. L. R. Rogers	Quartermaster
H.Q Company	
Major A. E. P. Bawden	Company Commander
Lieut. J. F. Drake	Second-in-Command
A Company	
Major J. Schofield, M.C.	Company Commander
Capt. H. D. Boyce	Second-in-Command
Lieut. H. H. Handley	O.C., No. 1 Platoon
Lieut. T. R. Thompson	Platoon Officer, No. 1 Platoon
Lieut. J. Garner	O.C., No. 2 Platoon
Lieut. E. J. Dawson	O.C., No. 3 Platoon
Lieut. W. C. Witty	Platoon Officer, No. 3 Platoon
Lieut. W. A. Stevens	O.C., No. 4 Platoon
2nd Lt. C. C. Oakham	Platoon Officer, No. 1 Platoon
2nd Lt. R. N. Reading	Platoon Officer, No. 2 Platoon
2nd Lt. A. C. Gurney	Platoon Officer, No. 4 Platoon

Name and Rank	*Appointment*
B Company	
Major T. F. Muncey	Company Commander
Capt. R. H. Budgen	Second-in-Command
Lieut. R. E. Mitchell	O.C., No. 5 Platoon
Lieut. S. T. Lofting	O.C., No. 6 Platoon
Lieut. R. E. Crisp	Platoon Officer, No. 6 Platoon
Lieut. J. Kelly	O.C., No. 7 Platoon
Lieut. L. A. Jones	Platoon Officer, No. 7 Platoon
Lieut. F. W. Dowling	O.C., No. 8 Platoon
Lieut. S. L. Hollingshead	Platoon Officer, No. 8 Platoon
2nd Lt. F. Heydon	Platoon Officer, No. 5 Platoon
C Company	
Major W. O. R. Davies	Company Commander
Capt. C. W. Withers	Second-in-Command
Lieut. A. O. Elcoat	O.C., No. 9 Platoon
Lieut. E. G. Gates	Platoon Officer, No. 9 Platoon
Lieut. C. I. Birkbeck	O.C., No. 10 Platoon
Lieut. J. H. Bartholemew	O.C., No. 11 Platoon
Lieut. H. A. Chalk	O.C., No. 12 Platoon
2nd Lt. V. S. Maly	Platoon Officer, No. 10 Platoon
2nd Lt. F. W. West	Platoon Officer, No. 11 Platoon
2nd Lt. H. R. Tarrant	Platoon Officer, No. 12 Platoon
D Company	*Appointment*
Major C. King	Company Commander
Capt. J. Powell	Second-in-Command
Lieut. E. A. Edwards	O.C., No. 13 Platoon
Lieut. O. F. West	O.C., No. 14 Platoon
Lieut. J. Busby	Platoon Officer, No. 14 Platoon
Lieut. W. A. A. Paul	O.C., No. 15 Platoon
Lieut. E. H. J. Hancock	O.C., No. 16 Platoon
Lieut. E. D. Russell	Platoon Officer, No. 16 Platoon
2nd Lt. H. H. Lay	Platoon Officer, No. 13 Platoon
2nd Lt. R. C. Edwards	Platoon Officer, No. 15 Platoon
E Company	
Major W. J. Turner	Company Commander
Capt. H. J. Call	Second-in-Command
Lieut. H. Lampitt	O.C., No. 17 Platoon
Lieut. C. H. Owen	O.C., No. 18 Platoon
Lieut. H. N. Wakefield	Platoon Officer, No. 18 Platoon
2nd Lt. J. Clark	Platoon Officer, No. 17 Platoon

11 The 46th Battalion

THE tram and trolleybus staff north of the Thames provided the men for the 46th Batt. Mr. L. B. Hewitt handled the enrolments, and in all some 1,200 volunteers were posted to the battalion.

The first step to military control was the appointment of section leaders in each depot. District Inspector A. J. Coucher, M.C., D.C.M., an official of London Transport who earned a commission in World War I became Battalion Commander.

H.Q. was set up in the Manor House offices and remained there until the occupation of requisitioned property in the summer of 1942.

Following the appointment of the Battalion Commander, four companies were formed, the commands of which were allocated as follows :

A Company	B Company
Mr. W. Small	Mr. G. Davis
C Company	D Company
Mr. T. King	Mr. A. Hill

The appointment of the battalion 2 i/c was made a little later when Mr. A. J. Barker was chosen. When Regular Army commissions were extended to the Home Guard the Battalion Commander became Lieut. Col. and all the Company Commanders became Majors.

The four-company organisation was maintained without alteration until November 1941, and during this time the battalion passed through all the familiar training troubles of the early Home Guard. There were shortages of most things except enthusiasm and determination.

Of the many improvisations made before the issue of reasonable numbers of arms the tram and trolleybus ' rifles ' were amongst the earliest. Bamboo poles cut to the length of rifles and filled with sand to weigh about 9 lb. were used for drill by hundreds of volunteers. Some of the more mechanically minded men paraded with home-made contraptions, most of which had for their chief object some form of mechanical or electric device to go ' bang '.

By the end of 1941 the battalion, in common with the rest of the L.P.T.B. Unit, had shown a remarkable improvement. Zones were looking to the Board to allocate a proportion of their troops for general service. In early 1941 Platoon Commander F. Alder was given acting rank of Company

Commander, and took command of a composite general service unit for service in the extreme western defences of X zone. This company included platoons which, for operations only, were drawn from three other L.P.T.B. battalions. During this year many other platoons were allocated to tasks not directly connected with the defence of London Transport property. Amongst these were Holloway depot, which formed one-third of the mobile reserve of D.N. zone.

These forces, known as the 'Archway' Coy., because they were so near to the famous road of that name, were commanded by Acting Major Brown of the 43rd Batt., who was transferred to the 46th with the reorganisation. When county names were introduced, the 6th Batt. became the 46th County of London L.P.T.B. Batt. The reorganisation of the L.P.T.B. Unit resulted in the battalion organisation changing on November 1, 1941, to the following :

H.Q.s
Battalion Commander	Lieut. Col. A. J. Coucher, M.C., D.C.M.
Second-in-Command	Major A. J. Barker
Medical Officer	Major H. Fisher
Liaison Officer	Capt. F. Carron
Intelligence Officer	Lieut. H. G. Knowles
Signals Officer	Lieut. P. S. Tompkins
Quartermaster	Capt. C. Cook
Ammunition Officer	Capt. A. Rogers
Group Liaison Officer	Capt. L. B. Hewitt

A Company
Company Commander	Major Small
Second-in-Command	Capt. L. H. Froomes
Platoon Commanders	Lieut. J. Malster, Edmonton
	Lieut. A. McFadden, Wood Green
	Lieut. A. Sharp, Finchley
	Lieut. M. Lovett, Hendon (Trolleybus)
	Lieut. R. Manger, Hendon (Bus)
Platoon Officers	Lieut R. Brazenor, Edmonton
	Lieut. R. Stokes, Edmonton
	Lieut. H. Pike, Edmonton
	Lieut. A. Smith, Finchley
	Lieut. F. Mills, Hendon (Bus)

B Company
Company Commander	Major Davis
Second-in-Command	Capt. A. Large
Platoon Commanders	2nd Lt. A. Bedford, Stamford Hill
	Lieut. G. Hudson, Holloway (Trolleybus)
	Lieut. S. Adams, Holloway (Bus)
	Lieut. R. J. Dudley, Chalk Farm
Platoon Officers	Lieut. A. Fishenden, Holloway (Trolleybus)
	Lieut. J. Keightley, Holloway (Trolleybus)
	Lieut. A. Gillan, Chalk Farm
	Lieut. Clark, Holloway (Bus)

C Company

Company Commander	Major Franks
Second-in-Command	Capt. J. H. Dennis, M.M.
Platoon Commanders	Lieut. R. H. Harding, Enfield (Bus)
	Lieut. C. Saunders, Palmers Green
	Lieut. F. Evans, West Green
	2nd Lt. S. Daeche, Muswell Hill
	Lieut. G. F. Gibson, Tottenham

D Company

Company Commander	Major T. J. Stammers, M.M.
Second-in-Command	Capt. Wheeler
Platoon Commanders	Lieut. S. A. Thompson, Hertford
	Lieut. E. Bosely, Hatfield
	Lieut. H. J. Trussell, Luton
	Lieut. R. J. Kenyon, Potters Bar
Platoon Officer	2nd Lt. A. Bylett, Potters Bar

E Company

Company Commander	Lieut. H. A. Walker
Second-in-Command	
Platoon Commanders	Lieut. L. A. Simmons, Watford High Street
	Lieut. A. Johnson, Watford, Levesden Road
	Lieut. A. P. Hoare, Tring
	Lieut. A. Chapman, Hemel Hempstead

F Company

Company Commander	Major T. S. Munro
Second-in-Command	Capt. T. R. Bilbow
Platoon Commanders	Lieut. J. Dalton, Hendon Central
	Lieut. W. Challis, Hendon Central
	Lieut. G. L. Webster, Arnos Grove
	Lieut. C. P. Barber, Golders Green
	Lieut. S. Creasy, Stanmore
	Lieut. G. J. Valance, Cockfosters
	Lieut. W. T. Brine, Edgware (Bus)
	Lieut. L. J. Ellis, Woodside Park
Platoon Officers	2nd Lt. S. Davall, Arnos Grove
	Lieut. H. J. Bailey, Golders Green
	2nd Lt. S. H. Grimmer, Edgware (Bus)
	Lieut. H. Jarman, Woodside Park

Machine Gun Company

Company Commander	Major J. Cameron
Second-in-Command	Capt. G. S. Hooles
Platoon Officers	Lieut. F. Figg, Stamford Hill
	Lieut. H. E. Ashton, Muswell Hill
	2nd Lt. J. Kirk, Wood Green
	Lieut. A. Breadmore, Finchley

LIEUTENANT-COLONEL A. J. COUCHER, M.C., D.C.M., WITH HIS SENIOR OFFICERS

Edgware platoon was transferred from F Coy. to A Coy. in April 1942, while the two Watford platoons were transferred to the 60th London Batt. in 1943.

The operational role of the battalion called for considerable general service commitments which affected all companies, some more than others. A Coy. built defensive positions between Kings Weir, Newgate Street, Edmonton and Enfield, and changes in dispositions on this line called for many alterations to strong points and M.G. positions. The scattered layout of the unit was difficult to control, but was facilitated by the use of R.T. in the early days. B Coy. contained the 'Archway' Coy., which constituted a very useful mobile

striking force for the D.N. zone. This unit, which had been raised by the 43rd Batt., consisted of all the general service troops in Chalk Farm and Holloway bus garages and Holloway trolleybus depot, and was later strengthened by troops from Stamford Hill depot. The size of this force and its special training required extra administration. B Coy. was commanded by Major Davis in its early history, with Major Brown in charge of the mobile troops, an arrangement which continued until Major Davis had to resign through illness. Afterwards Major Brown commanded both mobile and static forces of this company. The sector used these forces fully on all exercises and regarded them as shock troops for service anywhere in the sector or adjoining areas. They were heavily armed and highly mobile.

Their varied training was largely in the hands of Capt. S. H. Adams, an ex-instructor from the Hythe School of Musketry, who was fortunate in the valuable assistance given in arms training by C.S.M. Green, of Holloway depot, and after his promotion, by his successor, C.S.M. Thwaites, of Chalk Farm. The zone commander, later sector commander, provided special training, two Regular Army officers giving lectures for officers and N.C.O.s. In addition, Scots Guards N.C.O.s were detailed as instructors in many subjects. This company was controlled in the field by R.T., for which purpose an efficient signals unit was produced by Sgt. Page, who later became battalion signals instructor.

D and E Coys. in the country area were operationally under the command of the local sub-areas and both were mobile. Their training called for all-round knowledge of fighting in open areas as well as street and town fighting.

The high allocation of machine guns to the 46th Batt. necessitated the formation of an M.G. company. Very few of these units were established in the London area.

The first battalion parade after the reorganisation was in January 1942, when 700 all ranks attended church parade. After falling in at Summers Lane, North Finchley, accompanied by the Group military and bugle bands, the battalion marched to St. John's Church, Friern Barnet Road. The service was conducted by the Rev. S. H. Garnett-Birt, M.A., and was accompanied by the military band. Col. Brook attended and took the salute on the return march. The battalion later received a letter from Col. Brook in which he said, ' . . . . I feel I must offer you my hearty congratulations on the splendid parade your battalion put up on Sunday. I was indeed impressed, not only by the fine muster, but the really excellent turnout and soldierly bearing of the men . . .'

The outstanding training item in the history of the 46th was their training camp. In May 1942, Capt. C. W. A. Wheeler sought permission to start a camp, and eventually permission was given to occupy some of the London Transport huts adjoining Stanmore station. Although there was no equipment, the camp was officially opened by Col. Brook on July 18, 1942. The production of the first essential equipment was largely due to the combined efforts of Major Cameron, camp commandant, and Capt. Wheeler, camp adjutant. Following a successful summer, the efforts of Col. Brook to obtain full equipment and bedding were finally successful. Major Cameron resigned during this first season and was succeeded by Capt. Wheeler, who received his majority on taking over D Coy., in addition to becoming camp commandant. Nine months later, on April 3,

1943, the camp became the L.P.T.B. Home Guard north training centre and was at once opened to all ranks of the 41st, 46th and 60th Batts. Additional training ground was provided which gave opportunities for field training classes. With the help of the 40th Middlesex Batt., a bombing range was completed, while during the last year a 30 yard full-bore range was provided within marching distance. Large numbers of men passed through this camp and received training in most of the essential subjects. During its life the camp was also used by Army Cadets of the City of London and the Friern Barnet Sea Scouts. Of the many companies who sent contingents regularly, A Coy. of the 46th recorded the highest percentage of attendance.

Of the many parades held by this battalion one of the most impressive was at the annual memorial service arranged by the British Legion, held at Hendon on the site of a particularly unfortunate blitz incident. The 46th always attended this parade, and in March 1943 Lieut. Col. Coucher took complete command of the parade which included all branches of the C.D. service, British Legion and Old Contemptibles.

Of the many cups and trophies in the battalion the two senior contests were the Brook Cup and the Johnson Cup. The Brook Cup, presented to the battalion by Col. E. T. Brook and competed for on an inter-company basis for all-round general efficiency, was won by B Coy. in 1943—Major A. Brown, and by C Coy.—Major Franks, in 1944.

The Johnson Cup for officers miniature team shooting, first competed for in August 1943, was won comfortably by B Coy.—O.C., Major A. Brown. The following year B Coy. were beaten in the final by F Coy.—Major W. T. Bryne.

In March 1944 there was a successful battalion route march, when some 600 officers and men paraded before the Sub-District Commander, Col. (later Brig.) A. H. C. Swinton, M.C.

In April Sgt. J. Orr, Scots Guards, was appointed P.S.I. to the battalion and filled a long-felt want in the matter of training. The year 1944 will also be remembered by the 46th for the 'incident' at the great City of London test exercise. The idea of this exercise was to discover whether the well-defended areas of the city could be adequately held. It was announced in the Press that on the Sunday in question the area of operations would be closed to the public. 'It occurred to Major J. C. Malster of the 46th that some lessons could be learnt at this great contest which might be of benefit to the battalion. His application, made through B.H.Q., to the City Home Guard for permission to witness the exercise was not granted. Major Malster and the battalion Intelligence Officer—Capt. F. J. Carron, decided that there must have been some mistake, but there seemed no reason why they should not themselves test the city defences. Having reported their suggestion to their C.O., and received his ' blessing ', together with a warning ' not to get into trouble ', the two officers set off in full uniform and field service caps. The defence were known to be wearing helmets. Bearing in mind their C.O.'s good advice, they recalled that he had said nothing about making trouble for someone else. They found the area heavily defended by Home Guards, even to the use of manholes and sewers. After several abortive attempts, they entered a blitzed building, and by crawling through several similar buildings

they finally found themselves inside the main defences. Coming round a corner, they came upon an N.C.O. in charge of a M.G. and team. The N.C.O., turning round, seemed doubtful, and for a second the position was most uncertain. The spell was broken by Major Malster walking straight up to the N.C.O. and dressing him down for not keeping a better lookout. The sergeant saluted and apologised, whereupon the Major asked what area was being defended and received a detailed reply. The N.C.O. was then told again to be more careful as there were spies about !

They now walked round the defences and asked for and obtained more information, finally coming upon a field dressing station, complete with nurses and ambulances. To this day Capt. Carron attributes their undoing to the Major's interest in the nurses. Having stayed too long watching the first-aid work, a particularly robust Sgt.-Major passed and saluted, paused and came back and saluted again—walked away and studied them at a distance and then advanced again.

This was too much for the Major's sense of humour. In a moment there was pandemonium, the Sgt.-Major shouting for assis-

tance, which quickly came from all directions. A fleeting thought of resistance for the honour of the 46th was dispelled by the overwhelming numbers, and another look at the six-foot Sgt.-Major. Blindfolded and led away, they finally saw daylight before a number of very senior officers. Some were annoyed, but the defending C.O. took a lenient line and subjected them to a gruelling examination before finally congratulating them on their efforts. They were held prisoners for the rest of the day, but were taken to a point of vantage at the top of a building in Wood Street to watch the battle.

In July 1944 permission was granted to form an H.Q. company under the command of Major A. G. Rogers, and so the battalion now carried seven companies, an organisation which continued until stand down. This year was made notable by the instructions to train large numbers of Home Guards for C.D. assistance. At short notice a great switch round in training took place. The first-aid personnel, who had quietly pursued their way all through the years, now came into their own. Instructions in first-aid took precedence alongside rescue and demolition training by C.D. staff. The battalion had already seen much activity in the blitz and, with the arrival of fly-bombs and rockets, were ready to put their training to good use until, and in fact after, stand down.

The social spirit of the battalion was maintained successfully throughout its life. Many concerts and dances and two successful sports meetings were held. The liaison with other units and with units of the Regular Army and American forces was excellent. This spirit resulted in 78 officers and men of F Coy. being invited to an important U.S. bomber aerodrome. During this visit the American officers, N.C.O.s and men showed the greatest hospitality and did everything in their power to make the visit interesting and informative for every member of the 46th contingent.

The final stand down of the battalion was on Sunday, November 12, 1944, in the Victoria Recreation Ground, North Finchley. 470 all ranks paraded for inspection by Brig. J. A. Longmore, M.B.E., T.D., accompanied by Col. Brook, C.B.E., and many visiting officers. The brigadier particularly commended the guard of honour provided by A Coy. under Capt. McFadden—for, unknown to them, he had witnessed some of their drill movements before he had officially arrived, and judged more by this than by their appearance when they knew he was there. Following the address by the brigadier, Col. Brook spoke to the battalion and finally their C.O., Lieut. Col. Coucher, thanked them for their work, loyalty and comradeship. The battalion then marched away for the last time accompanied once more by the Unit bands. As they marched into Finchley trolleybus depot Lieut. Col. A. J. Coucher, M.C., D.C.M., took the last battalion salute.

The following awards were made to members of the battalion during its life

Commendation by G.O.C.
>   2nd Lt. A. J. Breadmore

Certificates of Merit
>   Major C. W. A. Wheeler
>   C.S.M. J. C. McCafferty
>   C.S.M. W. V. Johnson
>   C.Q.M.S. W. Morton
>   C.Q.M.S. G. A. Horn
>   Sgt. P. Turner
>   Sgt. G. J. Timson
>   Sgt. P. J. Silvester
>   Sgt. E. S. Brereton
>   Sgt. T. P. O'Donnell
>   Cpl. G. C. Slade
>   Pte. T. G. Lamb
>   Pte. W. J. West
>   Pte. G. Hunt
>   Pte. S. H. Taylor
>   Pte. R. Lovett
>   Pte. T. G. Palmer

BRIGADIER J. H. LONGMORE, M.B.E., WITH THE 46TH BATTALION
AT THEIR STAND-DOWN PARADE

ROLL OF OFFICERS AT 'STAND DOWN'

Name and Rank	*Appointment*
Battalion Headquarters	
Lieut. Col. A. J. Coucher, M.C., D C.M.	Officer Commanding
Major A. J. Barker	Second-in-Command
Major C. A. Royde	Battalion Medical Officer
Major R. H. Harding	M.G. Officer
Capt. F. J. Carron	Liaison Officer
Capt. C. T. Cook	Assistant Quartermaster
Capt. G. T. Akam	Second-in-Command M.G. Unit
Lieut. G. H. R. Hyde	Transport Officer
Lieut. C. J. Stones	W.T. Officer
Lieut. H. Whittenbury	Gas and P.A.D. Officer
Lieut. J. C. Malster	Intelligence Officer
Lieut. S. P. Tompkins	Signals Officer
Lieut. H. Harris	Asst. Adjutant and Press Officer
Lieut. H. Jarman	Pioneer Officer
Lieut. E. H. V. Botterell	P.T. Officer
2nd Lt. J. H. Barrett	Ammunition Officer
Capt. E. McCracken, Gen. List	Adjutant
Capt. E. J. Bates, The Loyal Regt.	Quartermaster
H.Q. Company	
Major A. G. Rogers	Company Commander

Name and Rank	*Appointment*
A Company	
Major W. A. Small	Company Commander
Capt. A. D. McFadden	Second-in-Command
Lieut. R. J. Brazenor	O.C., No. 1 Platoon
Lieut. E. G. E. Stokes	Platoon Officer, No. 1 Platoon
Lieut. J. B. Kirk	O.C., No. 2 Platoon
Lieut. H. H. Cause	O.C., No. 3 Platoon
Lieut. W. H. Gair	Platoon Officer, No. 3 Platoon
Lieut. M. C. W. Lovett	O.C., No. 4 Platoon
Lieut. V. H. Fox, M.M.	Platoon Officer, No. 4 Platoon
Lieut. R. C. Goodrum	O.C., No. 5 Platoon
Lieut. F. W. Mills	Platoon Officer, No. 5 Platoon
Lieut. R. H. Manger	O.C., No. 5A Platoon
2nd Lt. A. C. Howard	Platoon Officer, No. 1 Platoon
2nd Lt. H. Pavey	Platoon Officer, No. 2 Platoon
2nd Lt. F. Cowan	Platoon Officer, No. 5A Platoon
B Company	
Major A. Brown	Company Commander
Capt. S. H. Adams	Second-in-Command
Lieut. F. A. Figg	O.C., No. 6 Platoon
Lieut. J. F. C. Keightley	O.C., No. 7 Platoon
Lieut. H. G. Green	Platoon Officer, No. 7 Platoon
Lieut. W. H. Clark	O.C., No. 8 Platoon
Lieut. R. J. Dudley	O.C., No. 9 Platoon
Lieut. A. Gillan	Platoon Officer, No. 9 Platoon
2nd Lt. H. W. Drabwell	Platoon Officer, No. 8 Platoon

Name and Rank	*Appointment*
C Company	
Major A. F. Franks	Company Commander
Capt. J. H. Dennis	Second-in-Command
Lieut. W. C. Ince	O.C., No. 10 Platoon
Lieut. C. Saunders	O.C., No. 11 Platoon
Lieut. D. Costigan	O.C., No. 12 Platoon
Lieut. S. C. Daeche	O.C., No. 13 Platoon
Lieut. G. F. Gibson	O.C., No. 14 Platoon
2nd Lt. T. H. McKinley	Platoon Officer, No. 10 Platoon
2nd Lt. W. J. Devo	Platoon Officer, No. 11 Platoon
2nd Lt. H. V. Crocker	Platoon Officer, No. 13 Platoon
2nd Lt. S. C. Stevens	Platoon Officer, No. 14 Platoon
D Company	
Major C. W. A. Wheeler	Company Commander
Capt. T. G. Stammers, M.M.	Second-in-Command
Lieut. F. J. Ferris	O.C., No. 15 Platoon
Lieut. S. A. Thompson	O.C., No. 16 Platoon
Lieut. P. Cottrell	Platoon Officer, No. 16 Platoon
Lieut. E. E. Bosley	O.C., No. 17 Platoon
Lieut. A. J. Ford	O.C., No. 18 Platoon
Lieut. R. J. Kenyon	O.C., No. 19 Platoon
2nd Lt. W. T. Ringham	Platoon Officer, No. 15 Platoon
2nd Lt. W. S. Seaman	Platoon Officer, No. 17 Platoon
2nd Lt. J. Le F. Dumpleton	Platoon Officer, No. 18 Platoon
2nd Lt. A. J. York	Platoon Officer, No. 19 Platoon
E Company	
Major P. C. Hoare	Company Commander
Capt. A. F. Chapman	Second-in-Command
Lieut. A. F. Smith	O.C., No. 22 Platoon
Lieut. A. J. Fleckney	Platoon Officer, No. 22 Platoon
Lieut. F. C. Betteridge	O.C., No. 23 Platoon
2nd Lt. J. Parsons	Platoon Officer, No. 23 Platoon
F Company	
Major W. T. Brine	Company Commander
Capt. H. F. Oakley	Second-in-Command
Lieut. G. A. Stokes	O.C., No. 24 Platoon
Lieut. J. H. Gadd	O.C., No. 25 Platoon
Lieut. L. G. Daffern	Platoon Officer, No. 25 Platoon
Lieut. L. J. Ellis	O.C., No. 26 Platoon
Lieut. H. J. Bailey	O.C., No. 27 Platoon
2nd Lt. W. H. Metcalf	Platoon Officer, No. 24 Platoon
2nd Lt. P. D. Ottley	Platoon Officer, No. 26 Platoon

12 *The 60th Battalion*

THE 60th, youngest of the L.P.T.B. battalions, was formed sixteen months after the others, and the manner of its formation was unusual.

In November 1940 a junior officer of the 43rd Batt., J. B. Woodward, was appointed Company Commander of A Coy. At this time the 43rd, commanded by Lieut. Col. H. K. Cleary, carried an astronomical strength of over 5,000, all contained in three companies. A Coy. had over 2,000 all ranks recruited from the Board's bus garages north of the Thames, and west of a line from Victoria to Holloway.

As the Home Guard progressed so did the liaison between the railway units and the general service battalions. This closer contact began to take shape during the latter part of 1940, when it was realised that London Transport had produced and trained as far as possible some 15,000 men all detailed for protecting its property and rolling stock.

It was at this stage that X zone in the north-west of London began to take stock of that part of this 15,000 in their area and who were to be seen each week-end in ever increasing numbers. By far the largest proportion were attached to A Coy. of the 43rd Batt., and negotiations were opened between X zone and Lieut. Col. H. K. Cleary. While conversations were taking place, higher commands were taking similar steps regarding the whole of London Transport's Home Guard units.

The outcome was an application for a percentage of these men to be released for the general defence of London as distinct from the immediate defence of London Transport property, and as a result some 7,000 men were allocated defence tasks all over the metropolis. Of this number some 850 were in X zone, including 500 in A Coy., 43rd Batt.

The command of X zone changed on February 19, 1941, to Col. P. E. Coleman, D.S.O., M.C., who was quick to see the potential value of a force which, by reason of the Board's assistance, was almost entirely mobile. These men, then in four battalions, were formed into a unified force by making them a composite battalion for operations, but leaving them with their respective battalions for administration. Difficult though this sounds, and indeed proved to be, the force was given an operational role in the Harefield district and subsequently proved able to reach and hold an area many miles from work and homes. The command of this ' composite battalion ' was vested in the Company Commander, A Coy., of the 43rd Batt. in the absence of an agreed battalion establishment. Thus the foundation of the 60th Batt. was made, although this was not realised at the time by those concerned.

The first order issued by C.O. of the ' composite battalion ' early in 1941 gives the organisation of the battalion which, like most of the Home Guard at that time, bore only a small relation to Regular Army establishments ; Home Guard commissioned ranks had not then appeared in Orders.

The headquarters of the battalion was at the London Transport Divisional Offices, Dollis Hill, and the following appear amongst the headquarter's staff : Adjutant, E. J. O'Neill ; Quartermaster, W. Barker ; Intelligence, R. H. T. Liveing and R.S.M., J. Wood.

Within a few weeks it was found that the R.S.M. was a signaller of considerable service experience. In February 1941, therefore, J. Wood was appointed Signals Officer with the rank of lieutenant. His knowledge and hard work, particularly when the 60th were later issued with R/T, earned him and the platoon a fine reputation.

Two companies were designated A and B.

A Coy., commanded by S. Carpenter, of the 43rd Batt., had headquarters at Willesden bus garage, with platoons at Willesden, Alperton, Middle Row and Uxbridge bus garages, 43rd Batt., Wood Lane railway depot and Hillingdon offices, 42nd Batt. and part of Neasden railway works, 41st Batt.

B Coy., commanded by F. H. Alder, of the 46th Batt., had headquarters at Stonebridge trolleybus depot, and its platoons were at Cricklewood and Harrow Weald bus garages, 43rd Batt.; Stonebridge trolleybus depot, 46th Batt.; Northwood railways, 41st Batt.; and part of Neasden railway works, 42nd Batt.

In August 1941 the battalion received more definite recognition. Major Woodward was gazetted Lieut. Col. and a battalion 2 i/c was authorised. Major S. Carpenter became 2 i/c and A Coy. then came under the command of Major E. H. Robertson.

By the autumn of 1941 the unit was well established as part of the north-west London defence scheme. About the same time Higher Command decided to reorganise the entire Unit on a zone basis instead of on London Transport's departmental basis. Seven battalions were needed, and so the composite unit was taken as the nucleus for the extra battalion. On November 1, 1941, the L.P.T.B. composite battalion ceased, and a new battalion, the 60th London, took its place in the line, still under the command of Lieut. Col. J. B. Woodward.

The two original companies were scrapped. The battalion, by reason of its complete absorption of all remaining L.P.T.B. Home Guards in X zone, and also those in the London Transport country areas bordering on X zone, now showed a strength of 57 officers and 1,737 other ranks.

Five companies were made and represented a compromise between the geographical situation of the properties which formed the platoon headquarters and the departmental divisions of London Transport. The organisation was : C.O., Lieut. Col. J. B. Woodward ; 2 i/c, Major S. Carpenter ; Adjutant, Capt. E. J. O'Neill ; Quartermaster, Capt. W. H. Watts ; Intelligence, Capt. R. H. T. Liveing ; Ammunition, Capt. R. Eyre ; Liaison, Capt. R. Gray ; W.T.O., Capt. E. G. Perry ; P.P.D., Lieut. L. R. Cotton ; Signals, Lieut. J. Wood ; P.A.D., Lieut. H. Monk ; M.O., Major A. G. Gilchrist ; and Assistant Adjutant, Lieut. H. J. McKay.

A Coy.—O.C., Major J. A. Tucker ; 2 i/c, Capt. W. C. Johns. Platoons—Willesden and Middle Row bus garages and Alperton station.

B Coy.—O.C., Major F. H. Alder ; 2 i/c, Capt. J. Pile. Platoons—Harrow Weald and Alperton bus garages and Stonebridge trolleybus depot.

C Coy.—O.C., Major J. Field ; 2 i/c, Capt. W. Cowan. Platoons—Hillingdon Huts, Hillingdon, Rayners Lane, Wembley Park and Willesden Green station.

D Coy.—O.C., Major J. A. Tyndale ; 2 i/c, Capt. W. G. Morris. Platoons— Amersham and High Wycombe bus garages, Rickmansworth, Northwood, Watford and Chesham stations.

E Coy.—O.C., Major E. Orsman ; 2 i/c, Capt. G. Grange. Platoons—Neasden railway works (complete), Cricklewood and Uxbridge bus garage.

Many platoons were thus acquired, but Wood Lane was taken away. All concerned were sorry to lose this very keen platoon which had worked hard in the Uxbridge and Northolt areas and won the inter-platoon battlecraft contest. The association, however, resulted in the 60th obtaining two officers who will ever be remembered for splendid and untiring work and who contributed in a large measure to the success of the 60th— Major J. Tucker, M.S.M., Batt. 2 i/c, and Capt. R. H. T. Liveing, Adjutant.

Several personnel changes were made in the 60th during their first twelve months, chief amongst which were the allocations of captains A. and Q on B.H.Q. staffs who were to be Regular officers on the general list (infantry). Capt. A. Cooper, who had taken over A duties (unpaid) from Capt. O'Neill, in December 1941, became captain quartermaster in July 1942, whilst Capt. R. H. T. Liveing (Intelligence) accepted the opportunity to renew his Regular Army commission and became captain adjutant in October 1942. Battalion transport officer, bombing officer and camouflage officer were

made in April 1942, the positions being held by Capt. E. J. O'Neill, Lieut. A. T. Stapells and Lieut. C. Hodge respectively, whilst battalion P.T. officers appointment appeared two months later, when Lieut. E. C. Nottingham received his commission. Intelligence was taken over by Lieut. C. Seymour. Lieut. H. Monk, P.A.D., called to the Regular Army in August 1942, was replaced by Lieut. W. W. Smith the following month. Battalion gas officer was not appointed until the following October, when Lieut. J. O'Flaherty was commissioned.

Since the promotion of Lieut. Wood the position of R.S.M. had been covered by acting ranks, but, in February 1942 a selection was made by examinations held at Regent's Park barracks by R.S.M. Yardley, of the Holding Batt., Coldstream Guards. This resulted in C.S.M. Mealing obtaining the appointment on February 25, 1942, the C.S.M.s at that time being Hickey, French, Glynn, Warren and Clarke.

Application was made in 1942 for authority to increase to six companies by the introduction of a headquarters company. This was agreed, and the company appeared for the first time in August 1942, commanded by Capt. R. Eyre. They took over No. 20 (S.S.) from E Coy. and formed platoon No. 22 Infantry, No. 23 Smith gun battery and No. 24 Signals.

In November 1942 Capt. R. Eyre was promoted major, Captain W. C. Johns, of A Coy. was transferred as 2 i/c H.Q. Coy., and Sgt. Goode, of S.S. platoon, was made C.S.M. Capt. W. Watts was ammunition officer.

One further regular attachment was made when, after considerable correspondence by the C.O., Sgt. L. Barber (Middlesex Regt.) was finally appointed battalion P.S.I. on September 15, 1942. The battalion benefited considerably by the work and thought given by this P.S.I., whose keenness in musketry training never flagged throughout his service.

Further changes came when Major S.

Carpenter relinquished his position as 2 i/c battalion on November 28, 1942, and finally left for work abroad in January 1943. Major J. A. Tucker, M.S.M., O.C. A Coy., now became Batt. 2 i/c, and A Coy. were, for the second time, commanded by Major E. H. Robertson, who had held the same position in the early ' composite ' days. Capt. F. Gibson became 2 i/c, A Coy. At the same time, Major F. H. Alder relinquished his position owing to ill-health. Capt. J. R. Pile, M.M., was promoted to major in command of B Coy. Lieut. J. Jones was promoted to captain and 2 i/c, B Coy.

In June 1943 Major E. H. Robertson relinquished his command of A Coy. His 2 i/c was promoted and Major F. Gibson took command of A Coy. from June 16, 1943. Capt. W. C. Johns, 2 i/c, H.Q. Coy., now returned to A Coy. to support Major Gibson, whilst Lieut. C. Ambridge was promoted captain and 2 i/c, H.Q. Coy.

In July Lieut. E. C. Nottingham was transferred to the command of Smith gun battery, and the position of P.T. officer was covered by the appointment of Lieut. S. C. Hall.

In January 1944, Sgt. C. V. R. D'Arcy of the 12th Middlesex Batt. was transferred to the 60th and promoted Lieut. and Camouflage Officer in place of Lieut. A. G. Hodge who had been called to the Regular Army in May 1943.

The appointment of Lieut. P. Price to Asst. Quartermaster in November 1942, marked an increase in establishment. In the following April, Lieut. Price was transferred to Assistant Adjutant, Lieut. McKay having resigned following his transfer to M.A.P. R.Q.M.S. C. A. Drabwell was promoted Lieut. and Assistant Quartermaster, and held the position until, owing to ill-health, he relinquished his commission in November 1944. C.S.M. Seed was appointed Lieut. in his stead and A. V. Diggins became R.Q.M.S.

In February 1944, C.S.M. G. E. Durr (Highland Light Infantry) was posted to the battalion as a second P.S.I., and both he and Sgt. Barber remained until after stand down. C.S.M. Durr helped greatly with the drill and training of the successful Brook Trophy Team.

The C.S.M.s at the stand down were :

LIEUTENANT-COLONEL J. B. WOODWARD, O.B.E., WITH THE SENIOR OFFICERS OF THE 60TH

H.Q. Coy.—E. Hutson, A Coy.—E. Smith, B Coy.—T. O. Mahoney, C Coy.—G. D. Glynn, D Coy.—T. Bingham, E Coy.—H. E. Clarke. A Coy. lost one of their keenest soldiers when C.S.M. P. Hickey passed away in December 1943.

The C.Q.M.Sgts. were : H.Q. Coy.—H. T. Hewson, A Coy.—T. R. Botwright, B Coy.—L. J. Jones, C Coy.—R. D. Davies, D Coy.—S. Carter, E Coy.—P. G. Willoughby.

Lieut. H. Monk, P.A.D. Officer, was the first Bandmaster of the unit military band. A large percentage of both the Military Band and the Corps of Drums were drawn from the 60th, including Drum Major Brown, and Drum Major Elles. Many will remember the band practice nights at the B.H.Q., especially the Adjutant who tried to answer telephone enquiries in the next room to the strains of Tchaikovsky's ' Swan Lake ' Ballet.

Battalion H.Q. was established at 260 Dollis Hill Lane, N.W.2. By October 1942, these premises were far too small and the following month H.Q. moved to 25 Shoot-Up-Hill, Kilburn, a larger place with the advantage of large gardens back and front. These premises were damaged three times by enemy action, and an A.A. shell burst near the cookhouse early in 1943. On February 19, 1944, 40 incendiary bombs fell in the grounds ; two set light to the premises and one entered the ammunition dump. The adjoining house and some dozen houses nearby were severely damaged by fire. The splendid work of the guard and A Coy. picket saved B.H.Q. These men were led by Lieut. A. T. Stapells and were commended at the incident by their C.O., the men concerned being H.Q. Coy : Cpl. Hardwick, L/Cpl. Gilbert, Ptes. Willcock, Herbert and Leek. A Coy : Ptes. Alder and Wood. On August 15, 1944, a flybomb fell on Shoot-Up-Hill damaging B.H.Q., A Coy. H.Q., and the Smith gun battery H.Q. Three men received slight injury. The gallant work of the battalion task platoon led by Lieut. A. J. Holloway has been referred to elsewhere.

The Pioneers under Sgt. Wilkes worked wonders at this headquarters, for many rooms were redecorated, and a 30-foot flag-mast was erected in the forecourt. This forecourt was made into a parade ground by acquiring ten tons of hard core and several tons of boiler ash from Neasden works, together with the loan of a steam roller from the local council. Battalion headquarters remained there to the last, but much other work devolved on the Pioneers when, prior to D-Day, the guards at night were strengthened to a full battle platoon. The Pioneers, now under the leadership of Lieut. Taylor as Pioneer Officer, built latrines and wash-houses with running water on the rear parade ground in a few hours, whilst three-tiered bunks were obtained from Willesden Council to convert many rooms into sleeping quarters. The Signal section worked equally hard and installed a complete internal self-operating inter-house telephone system. A London Transport telephone line was also brought into headquarters and maintained until stand down, although the necessary half mile of overhead cable was twice destroyed by flying bombs. H.Q. Coy. shared the headquarters with A Coy., who had no adequate place, but were ultimately given a house opposite B.H.Q. at 34 Shoot-Up-Hill. B Coy. headquarters remained at Stonebridge trolleybus depot throughout. C Coy. headquarters were always at Wembley Park, but were very cramped until additional accommodation was rented from the M.E.T. Athletic Association. D Coy.

were housed in a railway coach at Rickmansworth, whilst E Coy. had good accommodation in brick-built premises at Neasden railway works. Training space was always in demand in the winter months. To meet this an L-shaped hut was obtained from London Transport for the use of the Alperton bus platoon. Hundreds of hours were spent by the men of this platoon in levelling ground, putting in concrete floors for this training hut, and in re-glazing, re-felting and re-decorating inside and out. A brick building at 2 Dartmouth Road, behind battalion headquarters was later requisitioned to accommodate the Smith gun battery under cover.

The tasks allocated to the 60th were, from the start, largely dictated by their ability to move large numbers of men by road over long distances at short notice. This mobility had been encouraged throughout the battalion by their C.O., since the early days of the composite battalion and when at Harefield and later Yiewsley.

Trained to move rapidly by road as companies or as a complete battalion,

the 60th were made responsible for the defence of the open areas immediately surrounding Northolt Aerodrome, with a counter-attack role for the aerodrome itself. This important task was accepted with enthusiasm by all ranks. Week after week sub-units of the 60th could always be found exercising or digging in the vicinity of Northolt Aerodrome. Several times the battalion moved by road into its prepared positions at various hours of the day and night.

While Northolt remained the primary task, the 60th Mobile Battalion was introduced in 1944. It consisted of some 800 all ranks completely mobile and self-contained for service in the field for at least one week.

The unit was liable, firstly, for service anywhere in north west London as dictated by the Sub-Area Commander and, secondly, if required by London District, for anywhere in Greater London, and, finally, anywhere in or out of London—this last task, of course, only in extreme emergency.

The larger portion of the transport was provided by London Transport vehicles augmented by W.D. transport, private cars, motor-cycles and taxicabs.

By the time D-Day arrived, this force had given much time and thought to its training, armaments, and the packing and conveyance of equipment. Its fire power was considerable, especially in heavy, medium and light automatics. Considerable reserves of ammunition and food for seven days were carried in addition to iron rations, camping, medical and decontamination gear.

The first attempt at battalion standardisation of training and thought was started by Lieut. Col. Woodward's (then Major) lectures in the meeting room at Dollis Hill, Divisional Offices, in January 1941. Large classes of men, who had travelled considerable distances, attended courses on German tactics, anti-tank tactics and street fighting —these lectures were largely based on the Osterley Park Home Guard School principles. Then came more ambitious efforts—

zone officers were invited, including Lieut. Col. (then Major) Smith and Capt. Stevens, who were soon followed by Capt. Foulger (complete with knives), of Osterley Park fame. By June 1941, film training had been included consisting largely of showings of enemy uniforms and equipment.

As a result of contacts made with Capt. M. P. G. Howard, Adjutant, Regent's Park Barracks, in May 1941, the training of the battalion was for the next twelve months very largely in the hands of the Holding Battalion, Coldstream Guards. Records show small units of the battalion attending for training in June and July of this year, but in August, arrangements were completed by the C.O., for regular weekly training for the battalion. This very valuable assistance formed the basis of the 60th Batt. training until 1942. Training in all branches was provided at Regent's Park Barracks, in addition to a full week's course for selected N.C.O.s.

The kindness and patience shown by officers, warrant officers and N.C.O.s alike were an inspiration. Nothing was too much trouble and any subject asked for was specially prepared and laid on.

The training ground for one of the finest regiments in the world was happily shared by the modern counterpart of England's 'Trained Bands'. The sombre walls of Regent's Park Barracks must have looked down with astonishment at those early scenes.

The lessons learnt and friendships made will live long in the memory of all who attended regularly ; the lessons stood the battalion in good stead. Coldstream names that will not be forgotten are those of Lieut. R. C. Carr-Gomm, R.S.M. R. Britain, R.S.M. H. E. Yardley, Sgt. H. Kirk, and Sgt. H. V. Smith.

In July 1942, the training of the Home Guard by Regular Units had been placed upon a more official footing. Intensive training was instituted by Higher Command and fate decreed that the battalion should again be in the hands of the Coldstream Guards. Lieut. Col. W. S. Stewart Brown, commanding the 6th Batt. Coldstream Guards, and then attached to 33rd Ind. Guards Brigade, gave the 60th Batt. their first intensive Regular Army training.

The interest shown in the Home Guard by Lieut. Col. W. S. Stewart Brown was an example to all concerned, and the battalion benefited very considerably by the training received from those under his command. For twelve days in a fortnight during August 1942, the battalion witnessed and took part in the battle platoon training with a platoon of the Coldstream Guards. The demonstration platoon was commanded by 2nd Lt. Colville, an ensign younger by many years than most of the large number of the 60th who took part. This meeting resulted in many subsequent contacts when platoons paraded eagerly to receive instruction from this young officer who was esteemed and respected by everyone who had the good fortune to receive his training. The battalion lost a great friend and able tutor when

Lieut. T. F. Colville was killed in action on Christmas Day, 1942, whilst serving with the 2nd Batt. Coldstream Guards in North Africa under the command of Lieut. Col. W. S. Stewart Brown who was himself wounded and awarded the D.S.O. in the same engagement at Dj El Ahmera.

It is, perhaps, opportune to refer back to the 'composite battalion' to recall a feature of their training. During the first months of 1941, and before the call-up had touched the younger men of the London Transport then reserved by reason of their occupation, Lieut. R. Eyre, of Cricklewood garage platoon, organised a section of men who were selected solely for their ability to 'mix it'. Their methods of training were regarded at that time as unorthodox. Every man was 'tested' with four-ounce gloves and all selected equipped themselves with a killing knife, a strangling cord (cheese cutter), and a camouflaged suit. The care with which the knives were selected, sharpened and looked after reminded one of a Ghurka Regiment; in fact three men acquired

THE C.O. WITH MOST OF THE 60TH BATTALION OFFICERS

Ghurka Kukris and paraded regularly with them. They also trained for water obstacles and could be seen in St. George's Baths, Victoria, swimming in camouflaged denims, boots and helmets. The section was led by a particularly fit N.C.O. Sgt. C. Ambridge who led the section in their first appearance in a major exercise at Harefield, on March 30, 1941, when their methods of concealment and approach, combined with surprise and speed, immediately gained them the notice which they justly deserved.

In the latter half of 1941, the X zone commander issued an order to the effect that an S.S. platoon (special service) be introduced in all battalions. The men were to be selected from the toughest available and their task was to be first in the field and to lead wherever the going was hottest. The 'composite battalion', while not boasting a full platoon of such men at that time, could provide a fully trained section at once—it had been in being for several months. The platoon was commanded by Lieut. W. C. Johns, and later by Lieut. C. R. Ambridge, the original section leader. Photographs of this platoon in training reached various parts of the world, and letters regarding it were received by the C.O., from as far afield as Vancouver, British Columbia.

Early in 1943, the 60th were again in touch with the 33rd Ind. Guards Brigade but it was now the 3rd Batt. Irish Guards, under the command of Lieut. Col. J. O. E. Vandeleur, who provided the instruction. Lieut. Col. Vandeleur had always taken an exceptional interest in the Home Guard and the opportunities which he gave for training were always made with a thorough appreciation of the Home Guard's task and not a little understanding of their troubles.

The 60th were given regular allocations to send officers, N.C.O.s and other ranks for a full week with the Guards, and it was, indeed, always a very full week. Thirty-one officers and N.C.O.s attended these training

weeks. In addition, the 60th were fortunate in being included in intensive training and field firing with the 3rd I.G. during the 33rd Ind. Guards Brigade's visits to the West of England.

This Regular Army training carried out at Mortehoe and Woolacombe in North Devon in 1942 and Haverfordwest and Tenby Head in South Wales in 1943 was the toughest which the Home Guard experienced, especially the battle inoculation with plenty of live ammunition.

The Guards Brigade moved to other areas in September 1943, and thus ended the finest training the battalion could ever wish to receive. Of the Home Guard training within its own organisation, the outstanding feature of X Sector had always been the Hedgerley Park establishment. The facilities for all branches of training there had been steadily and systematically improved since the day this area became available to X Zone troops.

The 60th Batt. started to participate in the Hedgerley Park training in 1941 and the allocation steadily increased until, by the summer of 1942, the battalion were sending as many men as could be released for week-end training in camp and on the various ranges. The training by the end of this year included ranges for rifle, sten, grenade, M.G. and all sub-artillery. In 1943, the 60th twice accepted an allocation of half the entire camp at Hedgerley—an achievement in view of the high percentage of shift workers in the battalion. On the second of these occasions, the Corps of Drums accompanied the battalion, entertained the camp, and provided buglers for all calls. Retreat was beaten on the Sunday evening, after which the band led the battalion out of camp.

In addition to Hedgerley Park the 60th used the X Sector Spigot range at Northolt regularly. This came to be known as the 'Gaumont' range because it was on what was originally one of the Gaumont outdoor film sets.

In addition to Regular Army and X Sector instruction the 60th Batt., in common with all other battalions using Hedgerley Park, provided instructors from time to time. Not least amongst these was Capt. Perry, Weapons Training Officer, who was never happier than when dabbling with some form of explosive ; Lieut. O'Flaherty, who in addition to Hedgerley lectures built up the gas mindedness of the men with his team and the gas chamber at Battalion H.Q : Lieut. D'Arcy, who never failed to produce an absorbing field demonstration on concealment and field craft, usually with many ingenious gadgets ; and Lieut. (later Captain) Ambridge with his carefully thought out tactics and battle craft in addition to in-fighting, with or without arms.

Live grenade throwing commenced in April 1942, when ranges at both Hendon and Hedgerley were in regular use. All throwing was subsequently carried out at Hedgerley Park. Some 1,900 men passed through this training. The quiet efficiency and untiring efforts of Lieut. Stapells, Bombing Officer throughout the life of the battalion, will always bring back pleasant memories to those with whom he came into contact.

The battalion took full advantage of the allocations for No. 1 G.H.Q. Training School at Denbies, Dorking, and sent 38 Officers and N.C.O.s for various types of courses ranging from Battalion Commanders to Section Leaders. Twelve officers attended the Battersea Street Fighting Course. The South-Eastern Army Field Craft School at Burwash gave the 60th allocations for N.C.O.s on seven occasions, and these allocations were always much in demand. Many officers and N.C.O.s were also sent to the Weapon Training School at Purfleet, and ten to the Officers' School at Mill Hill Barracks.

During 1943, the battalion formed a Smith gun battery, which trained and fired as a battery. They were fortunate in obtaining an allocation for Chobham Ridges field firing during the latter half of this year, when they experienced their first battery shoot on field firing at direct and indirect targets. An opportunity was also taken at the same time to send teams from all companies to fire ' live ' with the Spigot Mortars and this was the first occasion upon which any battalion in X Sector had had such an opportunity.

Of the many exercises, those in which the battalion were given the role of the ' enemy ' always produced the best from all ranks. They were certainly at their best in the 'attacking' role.

Their first setback in a major exercise happened on December 14, 1941 in exercise 'Thruster', when movement by road was tried out for the first time. The battalion paraded 502 all ranks, and left base in buses and cars, according to orders, and proceeded satisfactorily until reaching Hayes via the Uxbridge Road. At this point the 'enemy', supplied by the 5th London, ambushed the leading company very successfully and a certain amount of confusion rather baffled a dozen umpires.

Less than two months before, on October 26, a force of two companies, provided by units of all companies, had achieved marked success when they attacked the Maida Vale telephone exchange. The G.P.O. Battalion responsible for its defence had apparently under-estimated the determination and cunning of the L.P.T.B. Battalion. A small coal shute was left open ! The umpire stopped the exercise within a few minutes and would have stopped it earlier had anyone been able to see through the smoke inside the exchange ! ! !

In January 1942, exercise 'Buick' in which Regular troops took part, enabled the 6oth to test some new dispositions in their battle area. 453 of the battalion were at battle stations round Northolt Aerodrome at 6.30 a.m. One of the very few ways of passing field telephone lines across Western Avenue was via a culvert under the road. This was always half full of water, often higher. The Signals Platoon made full use of this culvert but shorting in the line was all too frequent. During exercises, imaginary and actual, line breakages required immediate attention. Always the culvert was suspected and always Sergeant Woodruff, M.M. fell in, very often being submerged, but never sufficiently to damp his ardour, or to stop his work until the exercise was completed. Higher Command always gave us exercises in mid-winter.

The 60th appeared as an 'enemy' in an exercise on March 15, 1942 when they attacked the R.A.F. No. 4 Maintenance Unit at Ruislip. This was probably one of the battalion's fastest attacks. No exercise in which the 60th took part was received with such enthusiasm or will live so clearly in the memory as exercise 'Thunder'. It was with grim satisfaction that the battalion learnt that they were to attack their old 'enemy' the 5th London (of Hayes ambush!) during a test of the defences of D Sector, and few will forget some of the amazing scenes during the night and early morning of April 18/19, 1942.

X Sector had received an invitation from Lieut. Col. Whitall, commanding the 5th London Batt. to arrange an exercise to test their defences and to make the exercise of sufficient duration to allow the 5th an opportunity to try out their administration in conditions real enough to allow full police and C.D. co-operation.

Lieut. Col. J. B. Woodward was detailed to prepare and command the attack. His forces were to consist of the 60th Batt. A and B Coys. of the 12th Middlesex Batt. and S.S. Platoons of the 11th, 12th and 32nd Batts.

The 60th London Batt. detailed four companies : A Coy. including the S.S. Platoon, under Major J. A. Tucker ; B Coy. under Major J. Pile ; C Coy. under Major J. Field, and E Coy. under Major E. Orsman.

A Coy. of the 12th Middlesex Batt. was commanded by Major J. N. Green, and their B Coy. was under Major A. A. Sexton. The S.S. Platoon of the 11th, 12th and 32nd Middlesex Batt. operated under the command of Capt. H. G. Snelling of X Sector H.Q. The strength of this force was expected to be approximately 850 all ranks. Parade statements rendered during the exercise revealed well over 1,000 all ranks on parade.

The 5th London were responsible for Regent's Park and the area immediately surrounding. This included Primrose Hill to the north, Edgware Road and a large portion of the Paddington area to the west, and Oxford Street, from Marble Arch to Tottenham Court Road, to the south. This area, therefore, included the B.B.C., Paddington and Welbeck telephone exchanges, the power houses at Lisson Grove and Aberdeen Place, and several Borough C.D. control centres, one of which was contained in a Town Hall. The 5th London carried fewer shift workers than the 60th and, therefore, could rely on a normal parade state, during week-ends, of approximately 900. On this occasion they totalled over 1,300 all ranks, including the B.B.C. and affiliated units. Their orders were to commence mustering before dusk on Saturday, April 18, and not to stand down until a time which would be indicated late on Sunday, April 19.

Full emergency feeding and cooking was to be carried out by the 5th London during the whole exercise and all reliefs and battle and administrative orders were to be tested to the full. It was agreed that fifth column activities would be included during the exercise and all units could use this method of obtaining information (if possible) before the exercise. The narrative stated that large forces of 'enemy' troops had landed north of London and at 5.0 p.m. on Saturday, April 18, were within two to three miles of D Sector perimeter at several points.

Briefly, the object of the enemy was to disrupt communications and essential services, by attacking telephone exchanges, power houses, C.D. control centres, B.B.C., and Primrose Hill reservoir before finally consolidating in Regent's Park and holding the place long enough to allow imaginary air-borne reinforcements to land.

The C.O. 60th required his B.H.Q., with A and E Coys. of the 60th, to occupy positions in the vicinity of the B.B.C., by slow infiltration throughout the night and be ready to strike from inside the area at dawn, whilst the remainder assembled at suitable points on the perimeter and synchronised their attack at the same time. Many are the tales which can be told of men in all classes of attire strolling the streets or apparently musing in the taverns of the 5th London area during the evenings of the next few days.

As dusk fell on April 18, numbers of the 60th, now in full battle order, could have been seen in various districts outside the area of operation. An hour later B.H.Q. opened in Great Portland Street, and by midnight over 200 officers and men had reached the same premises by every known means. A few were caught, but the defenders did not apparently suspect this enemy H.Q. in their midst. Many anxious moments were spent when identifying and admitting the ghostly figures who reported all through the night. The greatest shock came when it was realised that the Battalion M.O. had inadvertently enquired the way of one of the defenders. It subsequently transpired that neither had realised who the other was in the black-out.

At the same time A Coy. of the 60th had established themselves by the same infiltration methods in Little Titchfield Street, and when nearly at full strength were unwittingly given away by one man.

Just before dawn, the remainder of the attacking force were on their starting line, except the 60th S.S. who were already causing a diversion in the Marylebone district. Records do not indicate whether the sudden appearance of smoke (which subsequently proved to be canisters) and the arrival of the fire-brigade—which closed a road of temporary importance to the defenders—was merely coincidence or conceived in the minds of the S.S. Platoon. From now on things happened with a rapidity which surprised both sides. Telephone exchanges and C.D. Headquarters were taken in quick time after real hand-to-hand encounters, but the power stations held out.

The S.S. Platoon reached the roof of the Langham Hotel from adjoining property and proceeded to take the place in orthodox street fighting drill from the roof downwards. The B.B.C. building itself was a very different proposition, but one man, Corporal C. Whiteman, by using a taxi-cab, contrived to reach what appeared to be a coal-shute and finally appeared in the main hall of the B.B.C. The fortunes of the remaining units varied and street fighting of no mean order astounded pedestrians at numerous points, not least in the Marylebone Road and Clarence Gate area (B Company), where flower pots were dropped on the attackers from various buildings, fortunately without injury except to tempers. Some will always remember the scene on the steps of the Langham Hotel during the 5th London counter-attack, when the chief umpire—General Sir Guy Williams—endeavoured to make both sides temporarily cease fire before some, or all, became very real casualties. The 60th effected their consolidation in Regent's Park.

During the winter of 1942/3, numerous company exercises were held both by day and night and often in conjunction with C.D. services. Administration was tested by paper exercises from platoon and company level to large-scale exercises embracing all London.

A Coy. took an exceptional interest in their Northolt task. Their position in and around Gutteridge Wood necessitated a large amount of digging and wiring. Their large allocation of Spigot mortars required the construction of circular trenches with a centre island on which to mount the mortar. The revetting of this type of trench called for constant attention by week-end fatigues. Much detail and attention was given to field cooking and this company regularly provided hot meals for all ranks when in their battle area. The good work of their cooks was never more appreciated than when, after marching through the night from Ladbroke Grove to Northolt, led by their Colonel, they found steaming dixies and hot drinks ready and waiting in the early hours.

B Coy. were fortunate in having ready-made cooking facilities for part of their company in the Breakspear Cleansing Station. By the generosity of the C.D. they were able to use this station for periodical week-end camps and exercises.

C Coy., under Major Field, held several night ops. Probably the best of these was on October 17, 1942, when a very high percentage of the company were out all night on an exercise which had for its main lesson concealment and movement without sound. Their success may be judged from the discomfort of the Colonel who nearly trod on Lieut. Ward when stepping off the road to demand where the blazes that officer had gone.

H.Q. Coy. also made excellent use of the facilities at Major Farm, Ickenham. Mr. D. Poole kindly allowed the battalion the full run of his attractive house and grounds. Himself a Home Guard, Mr. Poole knew the problems of establishing battalion battle H.Q. and generously placed several rooms and most of the out-buildings at the disposal of the battalion. Two field telephone exchanges were installed, in addition to direct lines to Northolt Aerodrome. H.Q. Coy. constructed brick ovens, and an ammunition dump was built in the orchard. More than once the drawing room was converted into a control room for major exercises. Night exercises caused complete upheaval in this quiet menage and always resulted in a smiling Mrs. Poole appearing at all hours with hot drinks.

The greatest muster of the battalion was on the occasion of exercise 'Gadfly'. This long-awaited test mobilisation of all Home Guards, without undue interference with their civil employment, came in the early hours of October 24, 1943. Despite considerable fog, the 60th, during that morning, paraded 1,132 all ranks. Many had to be released for work but many were still reporting when the exercise stopped at midday. This parade was one of which the 60th were always particularly proud.

In common with most L.P.T.B. battalions, the 60th had one very scattered company. In the country area outside the London boundary D Coy. were, therefore, the only company not directly attached to the battalion for operations. Originally formed in six platoons reaching a 16-mile semi-circle from High Wycombe to Watford, they were later increased to eight platoons, by the total transfer of both the Watford bus garage units from the 46th to the 60th Batt. They received much help from the battalions of the Herts and Bucks Home Guard with whom they were to operate in battle. This included the provision of training instructors and rifle and bombing ranges. This company were in all battalion marches and parades despite the considerable distances which all ranks had to travel on these occasions ; several were held in foul weather.

D Coy. took part in many exercises in which the remainder of the battalion were not concerned. One exception was the north-west London Sub-District exercise ' Unique ', on April 18, 1943, when D Coy. found themselves as part of the ' enemy ' to the rest of the 60th Batt. who were at their battle positions at Northolt. This exercise required the 60th London to reach their battle area quickly with full transport. They arrived in good order 600 strong, with all weapons and equipment and found themselves almost immediately engaged on the northern flank by the ' enemy ' who turned out to be the 60th's Instructors— 3rd Battalion Irish Guards—led by their Commander. The speed with which Lieut. Col. J. O. E. Vandeleur personally led this battalion on foot across some eight miles of country taught all Home Guard battalions concerned very many valuable and costly lessons. It was a beautiful spring morning and much hard fighting was experienced, so much so that the greater part of D Coy. were ' wiped out ' in the outskirts of Ruislip and, therefore, able to adjourn to the nearest ' locals '.

On March 4 and 5, 1944, Nos. 12, 16 and 17 Platoons participated in the test stand-to of the whole of the Bucks sub-area. No. 12 Platoon (Amersham) were particularly fortu-nate in training facilities, having a miniature range next door and several full-bore ranges in the locality, together with a bombing range which they constructed themselves.

Sgt. Marchant of this platoon won the Donegal Medal for shooting, having com-peted against the Bucks Battalion. D Coy. won the Cup for the officers and N.C.O.s team shoot at Bisley in January 1944. This Cup was later put up for inter-platoon contests and won by No. 13 Platoon (Northwood) and later by No. 28 Platoon (Watford High Street.)

On June 6, 1944, the Allies landed in France and a few days later the Home Guard received urgent calls to help the R.A.O.C. in packing priority stores for the Normandy beach-heads. The battalion responded well to this call and gave over 1,143 man hours at Greenford and Northolt Park Ordnance Depots. Very many miles of signal wire, posts, pickets and fittings were bundled and packed by the 60th, often in record time. In this task all ranks worked side by side from the C.O. to the newest recruit.

The call from the R.A. for men to take over more of the London heavy guns on the Ack-Ack sites could not be answered in any numbers by London Transport as shift workers could not attend regularly enough for this work. The 60th, however, supplied 34 other ranks who were accepted for transfer to various gun sites in central and north-west London, where all of them saw action.

Neasden railway works and generating station, from which a large part of E Coy. were drawn, was constituted a Grade ' A ' V.P. which called for a special static defence force in addition to their considerable commitments on 'Downs Barn Ridge at Northolt. This force was transformed into the 60th Light Anti-Aircraft Troop in March 1944, under the command of their O.C. Major R. G. Orsman.

In common with other London battalions, the 60th were called upon to provide volunteers to train for rescue work at flying

THE 60TH TEAM AFTER WINNING THE BROOK CUP INTER-BATTALION CONTESTS

bomb and rocket incidents. Some 500 volunteers received training in various boroughs. This training was not in vain and the 60th attended many incidents both day and night over a very wide area and earned a good name for their rescue work, especially in the borough of Willesden. A single deck bus was placed at their disposal by the Board and converted into a heavy rescue vehicle, the equipment being supplied by the Willesden Borough Council. This mobile unit proved to be of immense value during the several occasions when the 60th were called out to incidents, particularly at night when sometimes a whole platoon was carried with the equipment.

Lieut. A. J. Holloway, of C Coy., and C.S.M. G. E. Durr, Highland Light Infantry and P.S.I. for the battalion, were mentioned in London District Orders in connection with their rescue work at one of these incidents. Numbers of men attended singly or in unofficial parties at incidents all over the metropolis of which no permanent record can be made. One, however, is worthy of mention. Capt. W. C. Johns returning from Home Guard duty, noticed that some of the outlying ammunition dumps of the Hyde Park magazine were alight as the result of fire bombs. In company with Regular Army and police volunteers he entered the area and worked very well amongst bursting S.A.A. ; during a rest period for a minute or two and while many fires were still alight, he decided to have a cigarette and had barely drawn the first puff when a highly indignant Sgt. Major hurriedly pointed out that smoking was in no circumstances permitted in the magazine area !

The 60th found little time for ceremonial in their training. Battalion route marches were only held at infrequent intervals. The battalion appeared regularly at Home Guard birthday parades. During both the parades held in the cockpit of Hyde Park the 60th were proud of their Signals Unit under Lieut. J. Wood and 2nd Lt. J. G. Fisk, who were made responsible for controlling the assembly of the seven battalions by R/T.

In 1943 at the first big London Home Guard birthday parade before the King, the 60th platoon were led by Lieut. C. Ambridge and Lieut. R. Collins of H.Q. Coy. whilst the platoon was drawn from various parts of the battalion. This march included much of the West End of London. On the same day X Sector held their parade in the Stadium at Wembley. The 60th Batt. were represented by their C.O. and some 300 all ranks. Eleven battalions were present with a grand total of nearly 4,000 and they appeared before a crowd which seemed nearly four times as large. The band of H.M. Life Guards provided the music and made the Home Guard march at a pace very much slower than anything to which they had been accustomed—the result was magnificent.

Many company route marches appear in the records. Battalion marches took place about every eight or nine months, with church parades in the interim. The first notable route march on March 1, 1942, gave the residents of Wembley, Hendon and Neasden a good opportunity to see the battalion on the march in full battle order.

The six-and-a-half mile circular route selected by the C.O. started from C Coy. H.Q. at the Metropolitan Athletic Ground, Wembley Park. The Corps of Drums of H.M. Coldstream Guards led this march throughout, the L.P.T.B. Group military band being in the centre of the column. Col. Brook took the salute from the steps of Wembley Town Hall. The weather on this occasion was cold and fine and excellent for marching. Very different were the conditions when the battalion next paraded for a route march on January 31, 1943. Drizzling rain throughout the night became steadily worse in the morning. Even so, the march was not abandoned and when the C.O. came on parade the Adjutant proudly handed over and reported over 400 all ranks, including men who had travelled some 20 miles to attend. The Group band and the Corps of Drums led the battalion, whilst the 43rd Batt. band took position in the centre. The salute was taken by Col. Brook outside Gladstone Park and opposite the road bearing his name. By the time the battalion arrived at this point two drum heads had given in and the musicians seemed to be blowing water out of their instruments.

The music continued, however, and the battalion marched past to the K.R.R. Regimental March and completed the full route with bands still playing. The next occasion, December 19, 1943, was when the battalion marched from Kilburn to Paddington and back. The salute this time was taken by Col. A. H. C. Swinton, M.C., Scots Guards, Commander North-West London Sub-District. The weather completely ruined what would otherwise have been a record parade for the battalion. Nevertheless, over 300 all ranks participated, together with the Group bands and the Corps of Drums.

In May 1944, the battalion was again represented on the anniversary parade before the King ; this time the 60th contingent was drawn from C Coy. and led by Lieut. A. J. Holloway and Lieut. L. A. Ward.

Of the various competitions in which the battalion participated the N.F. Cup organised by X Sector caused the greatest enthusiasm. The 60th first participated in April 1942, when a battle platoon was drawn from various companies. This team beat four battalions out of its ten opponents. In September of the same year, a team entered by H.Q. Coy. and led by Lieut. C. Ambridge all but won the coveted trophy. The teams entered by A and B Coys. in April and September of the following year were always well in the top half of the list.

The trophy presented by Mr. A. W. Snook, Acting Chief Engineer, Central Buses was competed for on an inter-company basis for all-round training in all classes of weapons. The Cup was held deservedly by C Coy.

A challenge cup was presented to the battalion by Mr. Barnes, a civilian living in the Harrow Weald district, who took a considerable interest in the local Home Guard. This cup became known as the Weald Challenge Cup and was competed for every six months to ascertain the best miniature rifle shot in the battalion. Pte. Tillyard of A Coy. won the first contest in 1943 with a score of 98 and was again successful in the first and second halves of 1944 with scores of 99 and 100. When Tillyard joined the Home Guard he had no knowledge whatsoever of the use of firearms and received his first elementary instruction in the use of .22 rifles at Baker Street range where he subsequently carried everything before him.

Owing to the restrictions on photographing troop movements only a very few Home Guard battalions have complete photographic records. The 60th are no exception, but during the last two years permission was granted to take a limited amount of film. This was made possible by the generosity of Mr. G. Harvey who very kindly lent his cameras. In conjunction with Lieut. S. O'Flaherty a successful film record was made which, when completed, showed for nearly half an hour.

To wind up its successful career the battalion paraded for its farewell march on Sunday, October 29, 1944. The indifferent weather which had dogged the 60th's parades, continued till the last but did not prevent 521 officers and men reporting.

Brig. A. H. C. Swinton, M.C., commanding North-West London Sub-District, and Col. Brook, addressed the parade after a brief inspection at the L.M.S. Sports Ground, Cricklewood. The battalion then marched through Willesden accompanied by the unit military band, the Corps of Drums and the Pipes and Drums of the 41st Batt. The column was accompanied by half a battery of its Smith guns, and the single deck rescue bus. The 60th L.A.A. troop mounted one of their guns on a lorry. The column was controlled by wireless, signallers being placed at convenient intervals through the battalion, the central control being at the parade ground and the saluting base. The Borough of Willesden erected a large saluting base outside Electricity House where the salute was taken by Brig. A. H. C. Swinton, supported by Col. Brook, Alderman W. J. Hill, Mayor of Willesden, together with the Deputy Mayor and Mayoress, the Town Clerk and C.D. Controller, Mr. W. T. Pirie, O.B.E., and many officers from adjoining units and local C.D. Controllers with whom the battalion had worked.

On December 3, the unit was represented in the great parade before the King by a detachment of 18 other ranks led by Capt. W. C. Johns of A Coy. and 2nd Lt. H. T. White of C Coy. On the same day No. 6 Platoon (Harrow Weald) of B Coy. provided a Guard of Honour at the parade of the 11th Middlesex in addition to sending 25 men to line part of the route. These men also mounted guard at Harrow Weald Garage and, with the 60th buglers, turned out to give a final salute to Lieut. Col. Moore commanding the 11th Middlesex. Major Levy, G.S.O.I., X Sector, in complimenting this guard, described them as one of the smartest and best disciplined that it had been his privilege to see during his four years with the Home Guard. Thus were the farewells made but few supposed that the battalion would parade again. Parade they did, however, six months later.

On June 17, 1945, the County of Middlesex held its Victory Review of the C.D. in Wembley Stadium. The 12th Middlesex and the 60th London Batts. were invited to send contingents of 100 each as a mark of appreciation for the Home Guard help at incidents. The 60th with the Corps of Drums and Buglers assembled at Wembley Park and marched with the band to Wembley Stadium; to the amazement of many onlookers who seemingly imagined that the Home Guard was dead. They received a wonderful cheer as they entered the famous arena for the march past. Lord Ashfield and Col. Brook were among those present.

After the parade and service they marched away with their bands and were dismissed at Wembley Park. They thus gained the honour of being the last L.P.T.B. battalion to parade as a unit and with a band.

The following members of the battalion received honours and awards for gallantry or good service :

Lieut. Col. J. B. Woodward   O.B.E. (Military)
Pte. E. Price   George Medal (Civil)
Lieut. A. J. Holloway   Commendation by the G.O.C. in London District Home Guard Orders.

Certificates of Merit : C.S.M. G. D. Glynn, Sgt. F. Woodroffe, M.M., Sgt. F. Seed, Sgt. E. A. Jerome, Sgt. A. E. W. Wilks, Sgt. R. C. Wells, Sgt. E. J. Cherry, Sgt. F. E. Langton, Sgt. W. H. Carter, Sgt. A. G. C. Browne, M.C., Sgt. J. T. McCullough, Cpl. H. C. Taylor, Pte. R. J. Elsom.

ROLL OF OFFICERS AT 'STAND DOWN'

Name and Rank	*Appointment*
Battalion Headquarters	
Lieut. Col. J. B. Woodward, O.B.E.	Officer Commanding
Major J. A. Tucker, M.S.M.	Second-in-Command
Major A. G. Gilchrist	Battalion Medical Officer
Capt. R. C. Gray	Liaison Officer
Capt. E. O'Neill	Transport Officer
Capt. W. H. Watts	Ammunition Officer
Capt. E. C. Perry	Weapon Training Officer
Lieut. F. Seed	Asst. Quartermaster
Lieut. C. V. R. D'Arcy	Camouflage Officer
Lieut. S. O'Flaherty	Gas Officer
Lieut. G. Seymour, M.M.	Intelligence Officer
Lieut. J. Wood, D.C.M.	Signals Officer
Lieut. W. W. Smith	P.A.D. Security Officer
Lieut. L. R. Cotton	Petrol Disruption Officer.
Lieut. P. Price	Asst. Adjutant
Lieut. A. T. Stapells	Bombing Officer
Lieut. J. Taylor	Pioneer Officer
Lieut. S. C. Hall	P.T. Officer
Capt. R. H. T. Liveing Gen. List	Adjutant
Capt. A. Cooper Gen. List	Quartermaster

Name and Rank   *Appointment*

H.Q. Company

Major R. Eyre	Company Commander
Capt. C. Ambridge	Second-in-Command
Lieut. H. J. Olive	O.C., No. 3 Platoon
Lieut. R. Collins	Platoon Officer, No. 3 Platoon
Lieut. F. Cornelius	O.C., No. 20 Platoon
Lieut. A. G. Chiles	O.C., No. 22 Platoon
Lieut. C. W. Nottingham	O.C., No. 23 Platoon
Lieut. J. Wood, D.C.M.	O.C., No. 24 Platoon
2nd Lt. R. S. A. Chiles	Platoon Officer, No. 20 Platoon
2nd Lt. S. S. Shea	Platoon Officer, No. 20 Platoon
2nd Lt. B. P. Basted	Platoon Officer, No. 22 Platoon
2nd Lt. B. C. Myatt, M.M.	Platoon Officer, No. 23 Platoon
2nd Lt. J. G. Fisk	Platoon Officer, No. 24 Platoon

A Company

Major F. Gibson	Company Commander
Capt. W. C. Johns	Second-in-Command
Lieut. F. H. Lugg	O.C., No. 1 Platoon
Lieut. J. Cann	Platoon Officer, No. 1 Platoon
Lieut. J. W. Housego	O.C., No. 2 Platoon
Lieut. L. F. Rice	Platoon Officer, No. 2 Platoon
Lieut. A. W. Wilgoss	O.C., No. 25 Platoon
2nd Lt. F. Robinson	Platoon Officer, No. 1 Platoon
2nd Lt. R. W. Bartlett	Paltoon Officer, No. 25 Platoon

B Company

Major J. P. Pile	Company Commander
Capt. J. Jones	Second-in-Command
Lieut. J. H. Purcell	O.C., No. 4 Platoon
Lieut. W. E. A. Cheape, M.M.	O.C., No. 5 Platoon
Lieut. P. H. J. Mant	Platoon Officer, No. 5 Platoon
Lieut. H. N. Burrows	O.C., No. 6 Platoon
2nd Lt. T. R. Daniels	Platoon Officer, No. 4 Platoon
2nd Lt. A. D. Morris	Platoon Officer, No. 4 Platoon
2nd Lt. W. R. J. Drain	Platoon Officer, No. 5 Platoon
2nd Lt. H. Herbert	Platoon Officer, No. 6 Platoon

C Company

Major J. Field	Company Commander
Capt. W. Cowan	Second-in-Command
Lieut. L. A. Ward	O.C., No. 7 Platoon
Lieut. A. J. Holloway	O.C., No. 8 Platoon
Lieut. F. W. Potter	O.C., No. 10 Platoon
Lieut. A. L. Crowdy	O.C., No. 11 Platoon
Lieut. A. C. Baker	O.C., No. 26 Platoon
2nd Lt. H. T. White	Platoon Officer, No. 7 Platoon

Name and Rank	*Appointment*
C Company (cont.)	
2nd Lt. C. McArthur	Platoon Officer, No. 8 Platoon
2nd Lt. R. M. Barnes	Platoon Officer, No. 10 Platoon
2nd Lt. H. Stimson	Platoon Officer, No. 11 Platoon
2nd Lt. A. E. G. Kennaird	Platoon Officer, No. 26 Platoon
D Company	
Major J. A. C. Tyndale, M.C.	Company Commander
Capt. W. G. Morris	Second-in-Command
Lieut. F. Witton	O.C., No. 12 Platoon
Lieut. A. V. Elliott	O.C., No. 13 Platoon
Lieut. E. J. Pickett	O.C., No. 14 Platoon
Lieut. C. J. Barkway, D.C.M., M.M.	O.C., No. 15 Platoon
Lieut. J. H. Glover	O.C., No. 16 Platoon
Lieut. A. W. Duff	O.C., No. 17 Platoon
Lieut. G. T. Barnes	Platoon Officer, No. 17 Platoon
Lieut. R. E. Strawn	O.C., No. 28-29 Platoon
Lieut. A. W. Askew	Platoon Officer, No. 28 Platoon
2nd Lt. B. J. Warren	Platoon Officer, No. 12 Platoon
2nd Lt. E. A. Jeffcoate	Platoon Officer, No. 16 Platoon
2nd Lt. J. C. McCafferty	Platoon Officer, No. 29 Platoon
E Company	
Major R. G. Orsman	Company Commander
Capt. E. Grange	Second-in-Command and
	O.C., ' A ' Troop 60th L.A.A.
Lieut. H. Wickens	O.C., No. 21 Platoon
Lieut. A. Skinner	Platoon Officer, No. 21 Platoon
Lieut. G. Whitley	Relief Troop Commander L.A.A.
Lieut. W. R. Payne	Relief Troop Commander L.A.A.
Lieut. F. W. Benson	Relief Troop Commander L.A.A.
2nd Lt. O. G. Jenkins	Relief Troop Commander L.A.A.
2nd Lt. A. J. Monk	Relief Troop Commander L.A.A.
2nd Lt. A. C. Furmedge	Relief Troop Commander L.A.A.
2nd Lt. W. Ward	Relief Troop Commander L.A.A.
2nd Lt. E. J. Townsend	Relief Troop Commander L.A.A.
2nd Lt. L. Twidale	O.C., No. 19 Platoon
Resigned, Transferred or Honourably Discharged	
Major S. V. Carpenter	Batt. i/c
Major E. H. Robertson	Company Commander A Coy.
Major F. H. Alder	Company Commander B Coy.
Capt. L. A. Simmons	D Coy.
Lieut. C. A. Drabwell	Asst. Quartermaster
Lieut. J. Hazel	O.C., No. 12 Platoon
Lieut. A. E. Johnson	O.C., No. 29 Platoon
Lieut. J. W. D. Kelly	O.C., No. 11 Platoon

Name and Rank   *Appointment*

Resigned, Transferred or Honourably Discharged (cont.)

Name and Rank	Appointment
Lieut. H. J. McKaye	Asst. Adjutant
Lieut. D. D. Menzie	O.C., No. 15 Platoon
Lieut. A. G. Sharpe	O.C., No. 3 Platoon
Lieut. H. A. Wickham	O.C., No. 7 Platoon
Lieut. W. D. Batchelor	O.C., No. 4 Platoon
Lieut. T. H. Fisher	O.C., No. 6 Platoon
2nd Lt. H. C. A. Haig	Platoon Officer, No. 2 Platoon
2nd Lt. F. Kennard	Platoon Officer, No. 4 Platoon
2nd Lt. C. W. Percy	Platoon Commander, No. 19 Platoon

Still serving with the Battalion in the Ranks, at own request

Lieut. F. C. Kerr	O.C., No. 9 Platoon

Called up to Regular Forces

A. G. Hodge	Camouflage Officer
C. Monk	P.A.D. Officer, Bandmaster
W. S. Hazelhurst	Platoon Officer, No. 6 Platoon

Deceased

Lieut. K. W. Tucker	O.C., No. 8 Platoon

13   *'Stand Down'*

THE order 'Stand Down' came to London Transport Unit, and to the entire Home Guard, on November 1, 1944. It was followed 13 months later by disbandment and the thanks of a grateful nation for duty well done. But that was not the end ; the Home Guard will be remembered as long as one member of it remains alive, and history will surely mention for ever the greatest part-time civilian defence force the world has known.

For those who served with the London Transport Unit the spirit of comradeship and self-help built up through the war years proved too strong to die. In the interval between stand down and disbandment there were many functions where members could meet. They ranged from concerts and dances with hundreds present to more humble, but just as keen gatherings for a drink and darts at 'the local'. In all of them the good fellowship between senior officers of London Transport and employees of much humbler civilian status was as noticeable as it had been when a rifle or a Sten gun was the sign of duty.

One function deserves special mention —a dinner given by Col. Brook and the senior officers of the Unit. Those present were :

Major General Sir James Syme Drew, K.B.E., D.S.O., M.C. (Director-General T.A. and Home Guard) ; Major General Viscount Bridgeman, C.B., D.S.O. (War Office) ; Brigadier General A. Symons, C.M.G. (Retd.) (Home Guard, London District) ; Brigadier C. Whitehead, C.B., C.M.G., C.B.E., D.S.O. (Home Guard Advisor, London District) ; Brigadier J. A. Longmore, M.B., T.D., D.L. (Deputy Director General T.A. and Home Guard) ;

Brigadier A. H. C. Swinton, M.C. (Commander, North-West London Sub-District) ; Brigadier H. L. Graham, M.C. (Commander, South-East London Sub-District.)

Colonel E. T. Brook, C.B.E. (Commander, L.P.T.B. Home Guard) ; Colonel G. S. Hussey, M.B.E., M.C. (Commander, L.M.S. Home Guard) ; Major Lord Denham, M.C. (London District H.Q.) ; Lieut. Col. L. R. Oake (Secretary, County of London T.A. and A.F.) ; Lieut. Col. A. W. M. Mawby, O.B.E., T.D., D.L. (Second-in-Command L..P.T.B. Home Guard) ; Lieut. Col. C. H. Smith, O.B.E. (Second-in-Command X Sect.).

Lieut. Col. T. H. P. Peerless (41st L.P.T.B. Batt.) ; Lieut. Col. S. G. Lane (42nd L.P.T.B. Batt.) ; Lieut. Col. H. K. Cleary, O.B.E. (43rd L.P.T.B. Batt.) ; Lieut. Col. T. H. Powell (44th L.P.T.B. Batt.) ; Lieut. Col. E. R. Alford, M.C. (45th L.P.T.B. Batt.) ; Lieut. Col. A. J. Coucher, M.C., D.C.M. (46th L.P.T.B. Batt.) ; Lieut. Col. J. B. Woodward, O.B.E. (60th L.P.T.B. Batt.).

Major R. B. Mason, Coldstream Guards (London District H.Q.) ; Major L. H. Hewitt (L.P.T.B. Home Guard H.Q.) ; Capt. F. E. Jones, M.C., and Capt. A. A. Horn (County of London T.A. and A.F.) ; Capt. R. E. Hawkings (London District H.Q.) ; Capt. A. J. Webb, Capt. A. E. Duffell, and Capt. W. Saville (L.P.T.B. Home Guard H.Q.).

Mr. T. E. Thomas, C.B.E. (General Manager, L.P.T.B.) ; Mr. John Cliff, (Member of London Transport Board, representing Lord Ashfield) ; Mr. J. Musgrave and Mr. Gibson (Richard Crittall and Co., Ltd.) and Major S. Foot, D.S.O.

The dinner was remarkable for the great praise bestowed upon London Transport Unit and upon their Commander, Col. Brook. It was stated that in the highest quarters the Board's Home Guard was counted as one of the most efficient units in the entire force. ' What a pity ' said an officer as he left, ' that all the thousands

who served could not hear every word. They would have felt proud.'

So we close the chapter but only history can complete the tale of the Home Guard. No one book could adequately depict this truly magnificent effort. It is a story which will forever colour the history of our island and one in which London Transport is indeed proud to have played its part. Proud to have been able to rely on such military strength which, from the start, made its foundation on the combination of age and experience in other wars with the youth and strength of almost another generation. Their discipline sprang from their loyalty to their King and Country, and as has been shown was taken and given without the slightest regard to the many considerable differences in their civil occupation with the Board. It would, I think, be difficult to find a more democratic Unit ; one in which so much responsibility was successfully handled by many who had little or no previous experience of leadership, and to whom such loyalty was shown not only by their colleagues in working hours, but also by those more fortunate in civil life, who when off parade were themselves officials.

Thus did they, like their forbears, give the world just occasion to marvel at these ' mad Britishers ' who, when brought face to face with defeat, seemed less aware of it than at any other time.

Those of us who knew the Home Guard will readily agree that the thought of possible defeat never seemed to enter any part of their activities. On the contrary, their greatest and ever-growing anxiety was lest they might not have the opportunity to face the enemy ; a grievance which resulted in applications for sections of the Home Guard to be sent overseas. This hope, that they might earn their ' spurs ' was cherished right to the very last day, and in fact is still their chief grumble.

May their memory live forever and may they never again be wanted.

FINAL HONOUR

THE final honour to come to London Transport's Home Guard was the selection of the Unit band to march in the Victory Procession through London on June 8, 1946. Word of the honour came only after disbandment and there was a mighty scurry to find all the men and set them to practising for the great day. This was an honour richly deserved as a glance at the section of this book which is devoted to the bands makes amply plain. It set the seal on the whole period of service of the entire Unit if only because it resulted in London Transport Home Guard having more men in the Victory Procession than any other Unit in Britain. A stickler for sound detail to the last, Col. Brook at once tackled the authorities for permission for the entire band to wear berets so that they would not be continually plagued by the usual ' fore-and-aft ' caps falling off as they played while on the march.

Lightning Source UK Ltd.
Milton Keynes UK
UKHW031240211020
371963UK00006B/209